TROLL
THE HUMAN BODY

by
Joan Western and Ronald Wilson
Illustrated by Michael Atkinson
and Michael Saunders

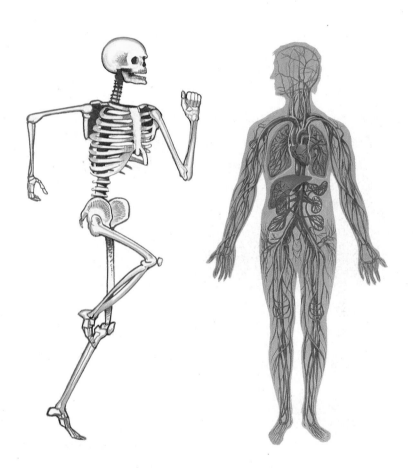

Troll Associates

Library of Congress Cataloging-in-Publication Data

Western, Joan, (date)
    The human body / by Joan Western & Ron Wilson; illustrated by
Mike Atkinson & Mike Saunders.
        p.   cm.
    Summary: Introduces the body's anatomical parts and systems,
including tissues and cells, skeleton, joints, muscles, blood,
heart, lungs, digestive and reproductive systems, brain, and senses.
    ISBN 0-8167-2234-X (lib. bdg.)   ISBN 0-8167-2235-8 (pbk.)
    1. Human anatomy—Juvenile literature. [1. Human anatomy.
2. Body, Human.] I. Wilson, Ron, 1953-   II. Atkinson, Mike,
ill. III. Saunders, Mike, ill. IV. Title.
QM27.W47   1991
611—dc20   90-38929

Published in the U.S.A. by Troll Associates, Inc.
Produced for Troll Associates, Inc., by
Joshua Morris Publishing Inc. in association
with Harper Collins.
Copyright © 1991 by Harper Collins.
All rights reserved.
Printed in Italy.
10 9 8 7 6 5 4 3 2 1

TROLL
THE HUMAN BODY

Contents

Introduction

Did you know that your heart beats about 100,000 times a day? Were you aware that your body replaces its outer skin about every fifteen to thirty days? Did you know that your brain is made up of about ten billion tiny nerve parts, or cells? Even the greatest, most complex machine on earth—whatever that may be—cannot compare to the human body. You could spend your whole life studying it and never know everything about it.

This book, however, will give you a good start. Here you'll read all about the human body parts you can easily see: arms, legs, skin, hands, feet, mouth, nose, teeth, ears, and hair. You'll also read about what you can't easily see, parts inside the body: bones, muscles, nerves, brain, glands, lungs, heart, intestines, and blood. You'll learn how each part works and how a number of these parts work together to form body systems.

In these pages you'll also read what proper diet and exercise can do for your body and how some drugs can help—and some others hurt—your body. And toward the back of the book you'll find a section on commonly asked questions and their answers about the human body, as well as a section on medical breakthroughs leading to healthier bodies and often longer lives.

So read on, and learn about a "world" more amazing than any science-fiction movie or book—your own human body!

The Body Systems

Our bodies are built to do many things. Some of them are things we choose to do such as running, swimming, or dancing. Others are things we do not even think about, such as fighting disease, using oxygen, or pumping blood.

Whatever we do, we use at least one part of the body, and there are many parts. They fit together in groups called systems, each with its own special job. The skeletal system, or skeleton, is the body's hard, tough framework. It is made up of many bones. It protects the softer inside parts and works together with the muscular system, or muscles, to allow us to sit, stand, or move. The muscles also help us control organs inside the body that we cannot see.

Our bodies need air and food to move, grow and repair themselves. There are special body parts to do the job of bringing air and food in from the outside and putting them to proper use. The digestive system takes in food and gets it ready to be carried where it is needed. The digestive system also gets rid of the solid wastes left over after the food is digested.

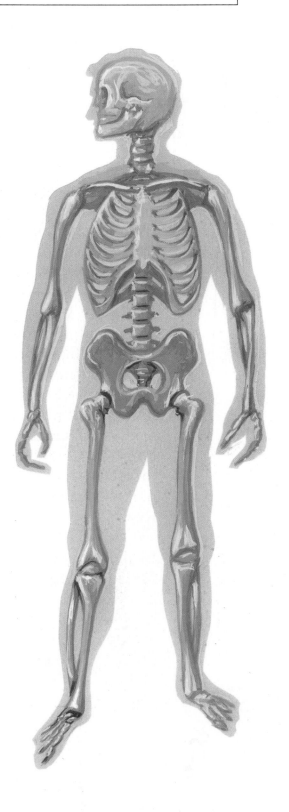

skeletal system

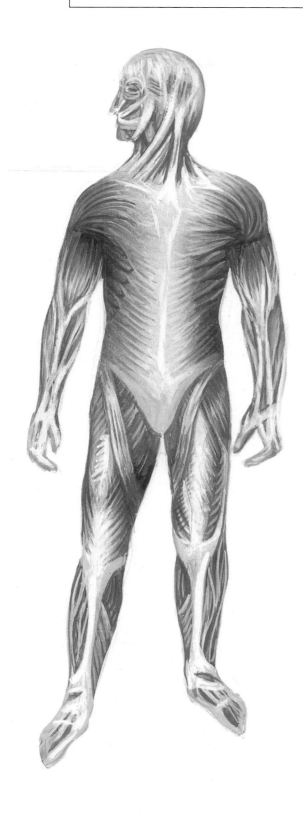

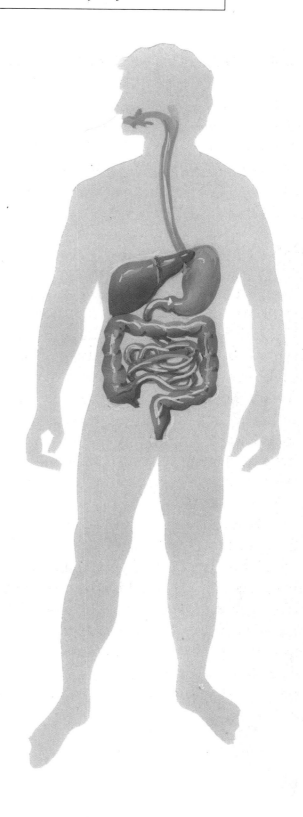

muscular system

digestive system

The respiratory, or breathing, system takes in air, draws the oxygen out of it, and releases carbon dioxide from the body. The circulatory system carries food and oxygen from these other systems to all parts of the body.

We need a special system to carry the liquid waste from our bodies. This is called the urinary system. Another very important system is the one used in having babies. This system, the reproductive, is different in males and females.

All these systems are controlled by the brain and the nervous system. Through the nervous system, the brain learns what is going on outside the body – whether it is hot or cold, whether it is light or dark, and even where a person is. Working with the nervous system, the brain tells the other body systems what to do. Because it functions as the body's control center, the brain is important to learning and understanding.

The brain and the nervous system are helped by a number of "messengers" called hormones. These are produced by the endocrine system. The hormones are chemical substances made in special organs known as glands.

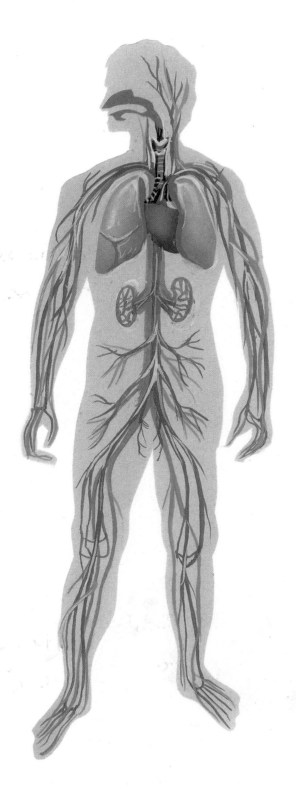

circulatory and respiratory systems

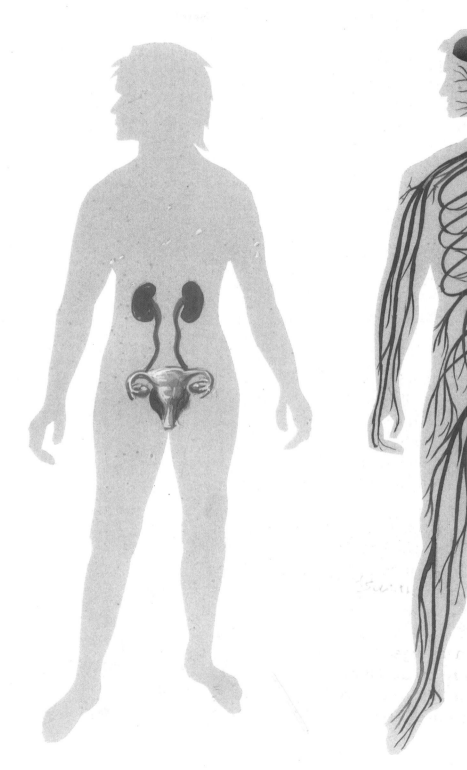

urinary system and
female reproductive system

brain and nervous system

Cells

The body, like all living things, is made up of tiny cells. Nearly all of them are so small that they can be seen only through a microscope. The first person to see a cell was Robert Hooke, an English scientist who was studying a thin piece of cork under a microscope in 1665. He described what he saw as tiny boxes, but in fact they were cells. A cell is the smallest complete part of the body.

There are several different kinds of cells in the body, each with a special job to do. Some parts are the same in all cells. Each cell has a control center called the nucleus. The nucleus directs the cell's activity and how it relates to all the other cells in the body. It contains important information in the form of a chemical code.

Parts of a cell

Nucleus – The nucleus of the cell controls the growth and work of the cell. It contains threadlike fibers called chromosomes and a round mass called the nucleolus.

Chromosomes – These are a netlike series of fibers inside the nucleus. They contain all the information the cell needs to reproduce itself exactly.

Vacuoles – Vacuoles are pockets in the cell wall that gradually move into the cell itself. They contain waste material.

Cell wall – The cell wall is the outer covering of the cell. It can change shape, and certain substances such as oxygen and water can move freely in and out of the cell.

Mitochondria – Mitochondria are one of the organelles, or "little organs," inside the cell. They produce energy for the cell with the help of chemicals called enzymes.

Different cell shapes

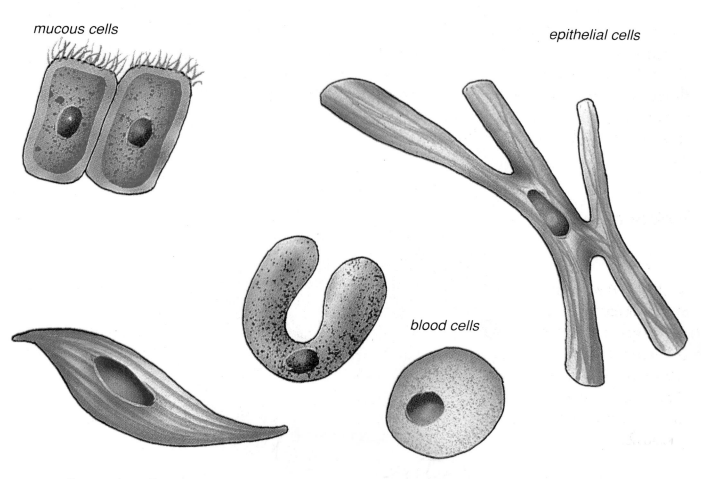

mucous cells

epithelial cells

blood cells

smooth muscle cell

The code determines things like hair and eye color. These traits, or features, are determined at the very beginning of a person's life.

Cells of the same kind, linked together, form tissue.

Millions of cells are dying all the time, but most are quickly replaced. New cells form when a living cell splits. Everything inside the cell is divided equally, making two new identical cells.

Skeleton

The skeleton of the human body is made of more than 200 bones. The main support of the skeleton is the backbone, or spinal column. The backbone is not one bone but a number of bones, all fitted neatly together. These bones are called vertebrae. (One of them is called a vertebra.) The vertebrae, like many other bones in the body, are cushioned from one another by a pad of softer material called cartilage. When a person moves, the bones do not rub against one another. Above the top vertebra, called the atlas, is the skull.

The main nerve cord, called the spinal cord, starts at the brain and continues down through a canal formed by the column of stacked vertebrae.

Attached to the backbone are twenty-four curved rib bones. The ribs form the chest cavity, which protects the heart, lungs, and the other important organs. Also attached to the backbone are two wide parts of the skeleton, called girdles. One is the shoulder girdle, made up of the collarbones and shoulder blades, to which the arms are attached. The hip girdle is formed by the hipbone. The hip girdle has a socket that fits the thighbone, or femur, the largest bone in the body.

The muscles of the body are attached to the bones. The place where two bones meet is called a joint, and it is at many of these joints that the muscles work to allow us to move.

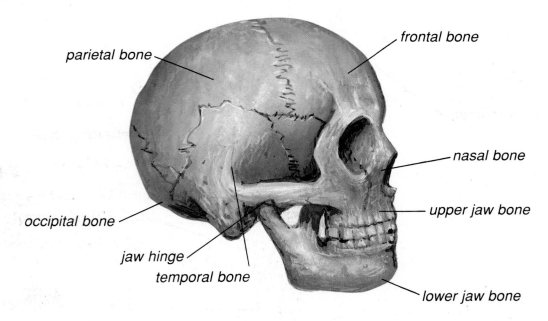

parietal bone

frontal bone

nasal bone

upper jaw bone

occipital bone

jaw hinge

temporal bone

lower jaw bone

The skull is a bony framework that protects the soft, sensitive brain and houses the organs of sight, hearing, taste, and smell.

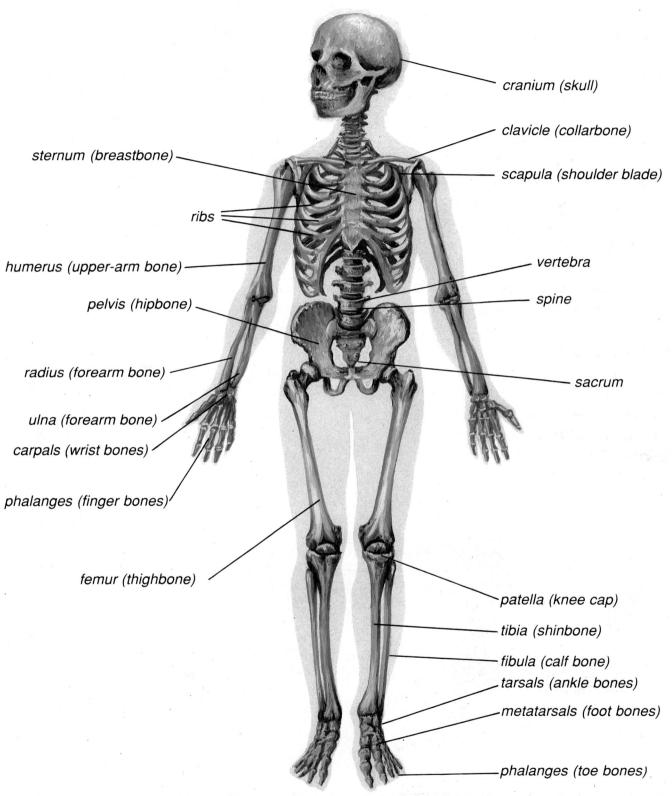

cranium (skull)

clavicle (collarbone)

scapula (shoulder blade)

sternum (breastbone)

ribs

humerus (upper-arm bone)

vertebra

pelvis (hipbone)

spine

radius (forearm bone)

ulna (forearm bone)

carpals (wrist bones)

sacrum

phalanges (finger bones)

femur (thighbone)

patella (knee cap)

tibia (shinbone)

fibula (calf bone)

tarsals (ankle bones)

metatarsals (foot bones)

phalanges (toe bones)

The skeleton supports the weight of the body. The bones of the skeleton fit together to allow movement.

Bones

Bones, although hard and strong, are living tissue. They need a supply of blood to continue to do their work, as do all the other parts of our bodies.

The skeleton is a framework of bones. It gives the body shape and protects softer, inside organs, such as the heart, brain, and lungs.

The long bones are wider at the ends. This helps make them stronger. They are filled with bone marrow, the soft, fatty core of many bones. The solid, hard outside part of bone, called compact bone, has a tough covering called periosteum. Under the compact bone layer is cancellous bone, which appears spongy.

When a bone breaks, blood between the break clots. Cells in the bone's outer layer increase, forming a layer of tissue over the break. New soft bone cells start to grow at each end of the break.

By the time we are fully grown, we have about 208 bones in our body. Our bones need to be strong to support us when we pull, push, run, jump, or lift. Long bones, such as the humerus (upper arm) and femur (upper leg) are wider at the ends, which makes them stronger. They are thin in the middle, where there is least stress and strain. This helps to keep the bones as light as possible so the body can move more easily. Although bones are made up of a variety of materials, such as marrow and calcium phosphate, bones are one-third water.

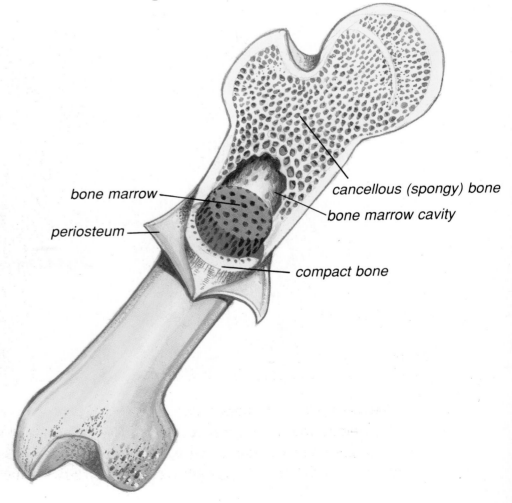

bone marrow

periosteum

cancellous (spongy) bone

bone marrow cavity

compact bone

Babies start out with more bones than adults. Some of the baby bones grow together to form a single bone in adults. A newborn baby's skull has twenty-nine separate bones with open spaces between the bones that cover the brain. By eighteen months of age, the bones join together to form a solid brain cover.

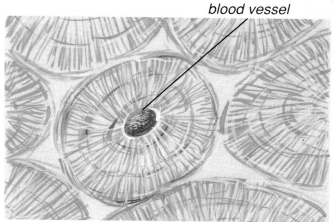

blood vessel

Bone is a hard, strong, living tissue. The dark area is a blood vessel.

The average size of a newborn baby is twenty inches (fifty-one centimeters). An average adult female reaches about sixty-five inches, almost five-and-a-half feet (165 centimeters) in height. This means the bones have a lot of growing to do. Near the end of each bone is a growth plate. This is the place where a bone grows.

Joints

Wherever one bone meets another, the two form a joint. Most joints are movable joints, but some are for protection. In an adult, for example, the bones of the skull do not move. They fit together tightly to protect the brain. This type of joint is called a fixed joint.

A strong material called cartilage separates the bones at each joint. Moving bones also have a kind of tissue called ligament that looks like and acts like a strap or cord. Ligaments connect to the bones and hold them firmly in place. Because ligaments are elastic, they allow the bones to move freely. Ligaments are also found in other parts of the body, where they help to hold inside organs in the right place.

There are five main kinds of joints. The hinge joint lets you move a part of your body back and forth, in one direction. The elbow is a hinge joint, and so is the knee.

The elbow also has another kind of joint, called a pivot joint, which lets you move your arm in a rotating motion. Another pivot joint allows you to turn your head.

Larger movements are possible with the ball-and-socket joint. There is one at the shoulder blade that lets you swing your arm in a circle. There is another at the hip that allows you to kick.

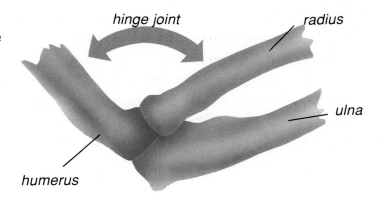

hinge joint   radius

ulna

humerus

The upper arm bone (humerus) meets the forearm bones (radius and ulna) at the elbow. This is known as a hinge joint because, like the hinge on a door, it allows back-and-forth movement. The elbow is also a pivot joint which allows the arm to rotate.

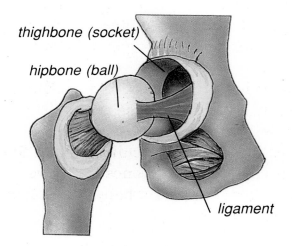

thighbone (socket)

hipbone (ball)

ligament

The ball-and-socket joint allows the leg to move in many directions. The leg can move forward, backward, sideways, and even in a circle.

The fourth type of joint is a gliding joint, such as those of the spinal column. Gliding joints are not for large movement, like at the shoulder or elbow, but they are enough for you to bend and stretch. The cartilage here is made in round pads called disks, which cushion the bone.

Inside hardworking movable joints, such as the shoulders, knees, and elbows, are special little pillows – soft sacs called bursae filled with a liquid called synovial fluid. The pillows cushion the jointed bones so that they do not rub against each other. Also, where two long bones meet at a joint, synovial fluid that is given off by a membrane between the bones keeps the joint moving smoothly.

The fifth type of joint is the fixed or immovable joint. These are at the pelvic girdle and between the bones of the skull. By the time a child is about five years old, the skull bones will have joined together, but a baby's skull bones are separated.

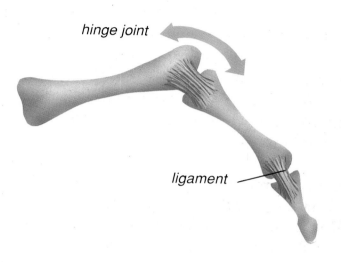

hinge joint

ligament

The joints between the bones of the fingers are called hinge joints.

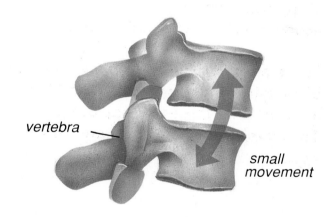

vertebra

small movement

The individual joints between the vertebrae allow only small movements, but taken together they allow the body to bend and stretch backward and forward.

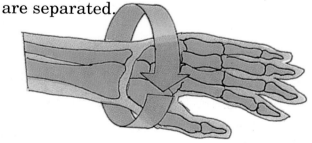

The pivot joint in your elbow enables you to rotate your hand up to 180 degrees. This joint helps you turn a doorknob or use a screwdriver.

Muscles

There are over 600 muscles in the human body. We need every one of them. We have three kinds, each with its own job to do.

Skeletal muscles are attached to bones and make the body move. Smooth muscles line the inside walls of many body organs, to help the digestive, circulatory, and urinary systems work. Cardiac muscle is the strong tissue that makes up the heart.

Muscles are made of millions of tiny fibers, or threads, called myofibrils. When they receive messages from nerve impulses, they slide over one another, shortening the muscle.

A single muscle does not act alone. Most skeletal muscles work in pairs, one attached to each side of a bone. One muscle shortens and pulls on a bone. The other relaxes and gets longer to allow movement to take place. Muscles never push. They do all their work by pulling.

When you bend your arm, for example, your biceps muscle shortens and your triceps muscle relaxes and gets longer. To straighten your arm, your triceps muscle gets shorter and your biceps muscle relaxes.

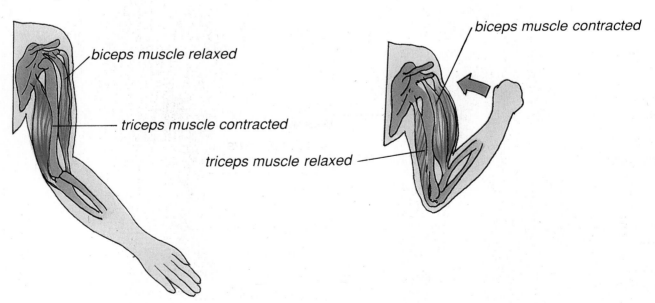

biceps muscle relaxed

triceps muscle contracted

biceps muscle contracted

triceps muscle relaxed

When the arm is straight the biceps relax and stretch while the triceps shorten.

When the arm is bent the biceps shorten and the triceps relax and stretch.

Skeletal muscles with different jobs have different shapes. Some are shaped like long straps. Others are more like flat sheets. Each muscle is enclosed by a covering that surrounds it like a bag.

Where this covering narrows and ends, it looks white. This is where it becomes the tendon, the fiber that connects the muscle to a bone.

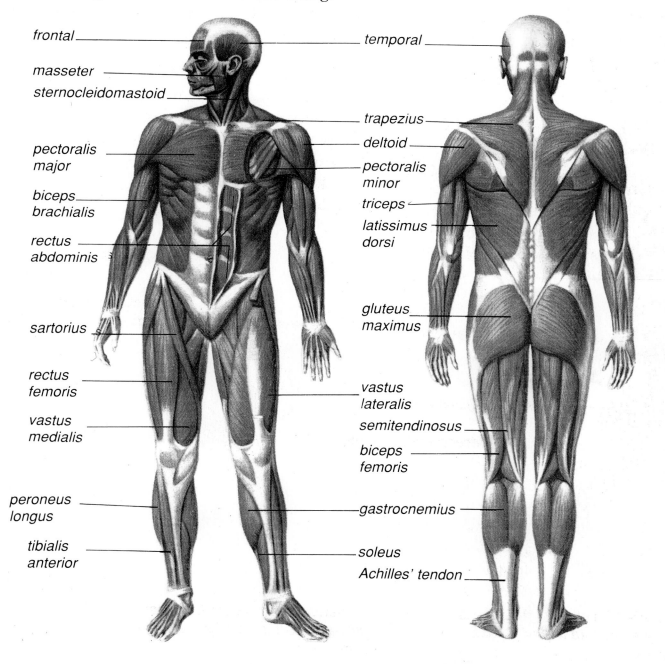

frontal

masseter

sternocleidomastoid

pectoralis major

biceps brachialis

rectus abdominis

sartorius

rectus femoris

vastus medialis

peroneus longus

tibialis anterior

temporal

trapezius

deltoid

pectoralis minor

triceps

latissimus dorsi

gluteus maximus

vastus lateralis

semitendinosus

biceps femoris

gastrocnemius

soleus

Achilles' tendon

The Circulatory System

Our bodies need energy to run smoothly and to help us grow and stay healthy. This energy comes from the food we eat after it enters our digestive system. We burn the nutrients in food, or oxidize them into energy, with oxygen from the air we breathe. It is the job of the blood system, or circulatory system, to get this food and oxygen to all the cells that need it.

The heart is a powerful muscle that pushes the blood through a system of vessels. The vessels that take blood to the body are called arteries. Those that carry it back to the heart are called veins. Arteries and veins are connected by a network of tiny blood vessels called capillaries.

The amount of blood in the capillaries helps adjust body temperature. Extra blood flows to the surface of the skin when the body is too warm, to carry away extra heat. When it is too cold the normal flow is constricted, or reduced.

The walls of the capillaries are very thin. Here, nutrients and oxygen can pass from the blood to every cell, where the food is oxidized. This provides heat and energy which permits all the body parts to work properly. Waste products, such as carbon dioxide, are passed back to the blood so they can be removed from the body by the lungs or other body systems.

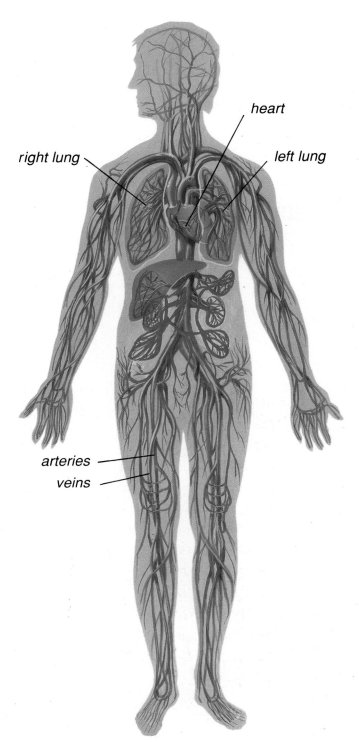

The circulatory, or blood, system (heart, arteries, veins, and capillaries) works closely with the respiratory, or breathing, system which supplies it with oxygen.

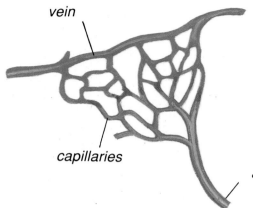

vein

capillaries

artery

The blood is pumped from the heart along the arteries. The arteries become narrower and narrower until they reach a complicated network of capillaries. The blood flows through the capillaries and eventually reaches larger tubes, the veins. The veins carry the blood back to the heart.

The arteries (shown here in red) carry the oxygen-rich blood away from the heart to the body. The veins (shown here in blue) carry oxygen-poor blood from the body to the heart. The lungs get the body's oxygen-poor blood from the heart and send oxygen-rich blood back, to start the cycle again.

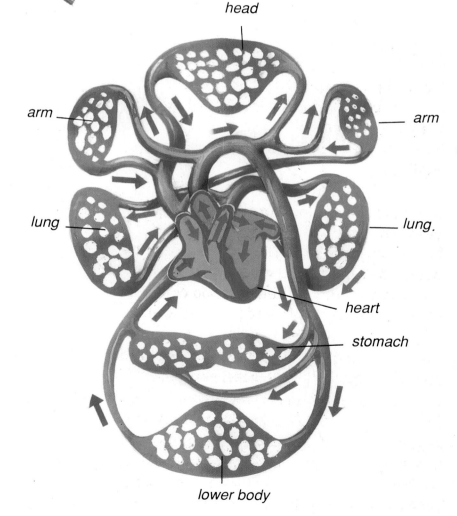

head

arm

arm

lung

lung.

heart

stomach

lower body

The Heart

During your life, your heart continuously pumps blood through your body. By the time you are seventy-five years old, your heart will have beaten about 3,000,000,000 (3 billion) times! All that pumping requires strong muscle.

The heart is really two pumps in one. One pump controls the flow of blood from the heart to the lungs, where carbon dioxide waste is exchanged for fresh oxygen. The other pump sends the blood to cells throughout the body. Each pump has two sections, or chambers, called the atrium and the ventricle. The pacemaker, a nerve center that controls the heartbeat, makes sure all four parts work in proper order.

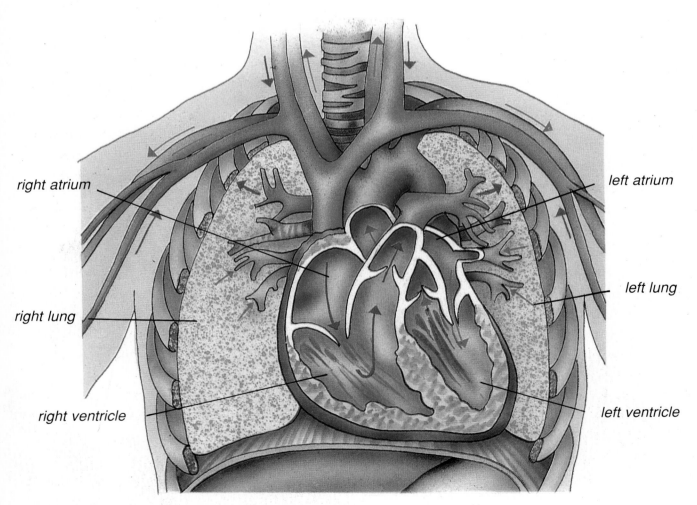

The heart is really a double pump. One pump sends blood to the lungs, to collect oxygen. The other sends this oxygen-rich blood to the tissues. The blood goes through a series of valves that open and shut automatically as the heart beats.

Blood from the body travels first to the heart's right atrium. This blood enters through two large veins, called venae cavae.

The blood is purplish in color because it holds carbon dioxide from the tissues. It flows from the right atrium to the right ventricle, where it is pumped to the lungs.

Once inside the lungs, the carbon dioxide leaves the blood and oxygen is taken in, turning the blood bright red. The oxygen-rich blood flows back to the heart, entering the left atrium. The heart sends the blood to the left ventricle, then pumps it out through a large artery called the aorta. The aorta branches off into arteries and capillaries that supply all the tissues of the body.

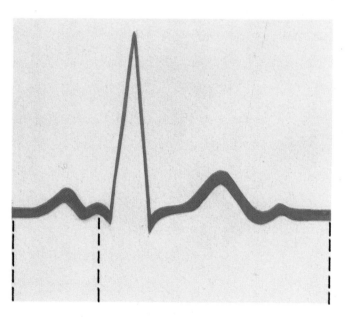

The pumping of the heart can be measured on a machine called an electrocardiograph, or EKG for short. This measurement looks like a wave each time the heart muscle pumps. If there are any problems with the pumping action, the EKG will show it.

1.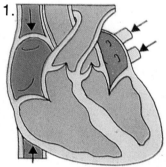

The cycle of the heart pump: (1) Blood from the body enters the right atrium; oxygen-rich blood from the lungs enters the left atrium.

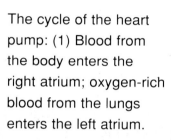 2.

(2) The atria contract, pushing the blood into the ventricles.

3.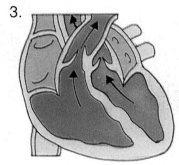

(3) Valves close to stop blood flowing backward; the ventricles contract, the new blood goes to the aorta to travel around the body, and the old blood goes to the lungs to pick up oxygen.

Blood

Blood is made of plasma, red cells, white cells, and platelets. About sixty percent of the blood is plasma, which is mostly water with proteins, sugars, salts, oxygen, and carbon dioxide. Blood cells and platelets are made in bone marrow.

Red blood cells, or red corpuscles, get their color from hemoglobin, which has iron in it. The hemoglobin allows them to carry oxygen through the body. A single red cell lives for about four months. When it dies, the bone marrow makes more.

White corpuscles, or leucocytes, fight disease. They reproduce quickly when bacteria enter the body to attack healthy tissue. Leucocytes leak out of the blood-stream into the tissue, where they do most of their work.

Different kinds of leucocytes do different jobs. Phagocytes get rid of bacteria and dead or worn-out cells by swallowing them. Lymphocytes make antibodies, which label intruders and lead to their destruction by other elements in the blood system.

Special blood cells in the bone marrow develop into platelets, which keep the body from losing too much blood from cuts, etc. When a cut starts to bleed, the platelets gather. Tiny fibers are made to plug the cut and make a clot, or scab.

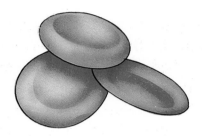

red blood cells

Mature red blood cells carry oxygen in the blood. They are disk-shaped and are flexible enough to pass through tiny capillaries one at a time.

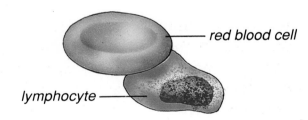

red blood cell

lymphocyte

nucleus

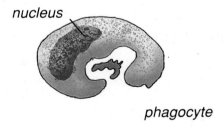

phagocyte

platelets

Various kinds of white blood cells do different jobs in the body. Lymphocytes carry antibodies to defend against infections. Phagocytes are white blood cells that swallow bacteria and other harmful particles. Platelets, another part of the blood, are needed for clotting.

Lymph

Lymph is a colorless, watery liquid that comes from the fluid that surrounds the cells in the body. Lymph moves around the body in its own system of vessels. Along the lymph vessels are lymph glands, or nodes. They contain millions of the disease-fighting white cells called lymphocytes. These contain antibodies which mark germs for destruction by proteins and disease-fighting cells in the blood.

Lymph is filtered in lymph nodes. Lymphoid tissue is found in the spleen, the tonsils, and the adenoids. Lymph vessels carry lymph in only one direction, toward the heart.

Lymph also carries digested fats through the body to cells that need food energy.

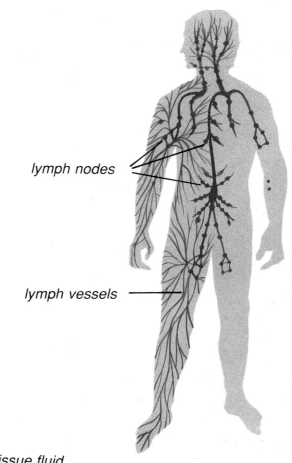

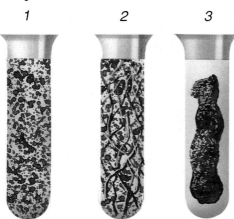

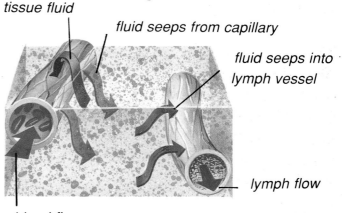

When blood is exposed to the air, it clots. The freshly shed blood in the test tube is liquid (1); but soon a tangle of fibers forms in it (2); and before long a complete clot forms and floats in clear blood serum (3).

Lymph is a clear liquid that seeps through the thin walls of blood capillaries and collects in lymph vessels. The vessels are spread through the body to form the lymphatic system.

The Respiratory System

We have seen that the blood carries oxygen from the lungs to cells that need it to survive. But the lungs are just one part of our breathing system, also called the respiratory system.

Our bodies need oxygen in order to burn the nutrients that we eat and convert them into fuel, or energy. The respiratory system carries oxygen down into your lungs as you breathe in, and then carries the waste gas, carbon dioxide, away from your lungs as you breathe out.

We do not have to think about breathing. Our body does it automatically. The average person breathes between ten and twenty times every minute. This is about 14,400 – 28,000 breaths a day. During exercise, it can be many more times than that.

When you breathe in, air passes up through your nose, or nasal passages, then down your throat and windpipe. On the way, the air is warmed and moistened inside your nose. It is important that the air is moist and warm so that harmful dust and bacteria are filtered out and do not go down into your lungs. Try blocking your nose and just breathing through your mouth. You will notice that your mouth feels cool and dry. If you only breathed through your mouth, you might suffer from sore throats and your respiratory organs would easily become infected.

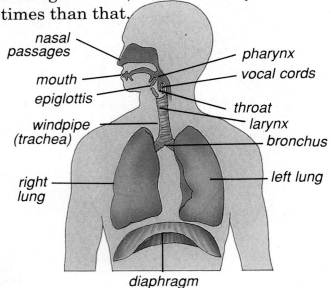

The respiratory, or breathing, system consists of the nose, throat, windpipe (trachea), and lungs.

nasal passages, mouth, epiglottis, windpipe (trachea), right lung, pharynx, vocal cords, throat, larynx, bronchus, left lung, diaphragm

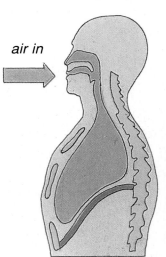

air in

diaphragm down

When you breathe in, the diaphragm moves down to allow the lungs to increase in size as they fill up with air.

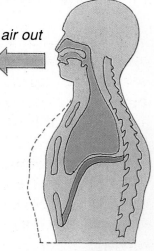

air out

As the diaphragm rises again, air is forced out of the lungs, back up the windpipe (trachea) and out through the nose or mouth.

diaphragm up

By breathing through your nose, you make sure that most of the dust particles and harmful bacteria in the air are trapped by hairs inside your nose or by a sticky fluid, called mucus, in your nasal passage and windpipe. The windpipe also has millions of tiny hairlike cilia. The cilia sweep back and forth, driving anything harmful back to the throat. There, it can be coughed out or swallowed harmlessly.

Lungs

Lungs are made up of spongy masses of tissue which are sealed inside the ribs by a thin bag called the pleura.

The windpipe, or trachea, which leads to the lungs, forks into two main bronchi, or tubes. (One is called a bronchus.) One tube leads into each lung, where it forks again into smaller and smaller bronchi and then into bronchioles, which are microscopic.

Lungs do not have any muscles of their own. In order to expand (when you breathe in), and contract (when you breathe out), they are controlled by the surrounding muscles in the chest cavity.

When you breathe in, your chest muscles pull your ribs up and outward and a domed muscle sheet, called the diaphragm, pulls downward below the lungs. The diaphragm, which stretches

from your backbone to the front of your rib cage, acts like an elevator, moving up and down. As the chest expands in both directions, the diaphragm moves downward and makes more room so that air is pulled into the lungs. When the chest muscles get smaller as they relax, the diaphragm moves up and air is forced out of the lungs.

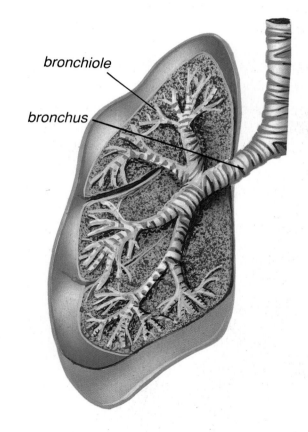

bronchiole

bronchus

When you are breathing normally, your diaphragm moves less than an inch. When you are doing vigorous exercise it can move several inches. You can test this yourself. Place your hands lightly over your diaphragm, just under your ribs, and take a deep breath. As your lungs fill with air, you will feel your diaphragm moving down.

While air is in the lungs, an important change takes place. The bronchioles end in bunches of tiny air sacs, called alveoli. (One is called an alveolus.) Your lungs contain hundreds of millions of alveoli. Every tiny alveolus is surrounded by blood capillaries. The walls, or membrane, of the alveoli and capillaries are very, very thin – much thinner than tissue paper. Through these walls, oxygen from the outside air passes from the alveoli to the capillaries. Carbon dioxide moves from the capillaries to the alveoli where it can be breathed out. This is known as the exchange of gases.

Although you have two lungs, they are not identical. Your right lung has three sets of lobes, but your left lung has only two sets, plus a small notch to fit the bottom of the heart. The heart and lungs work very closely with each other because the heart needs to have oxygen-rich blood to pump around the body. This oxygen-rich blood is carried from the lungs to the left side of the heart. Oxygen-poor blood, which contains carbon dioxide, comes from the right side of the heart, where it is pumped into the lungs ready to be breathed out.

The alveolus

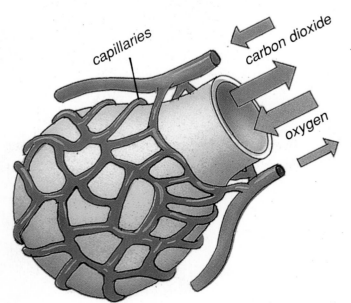

Air passes from the lungs into the bloodstream through tiny air sacs, or alveoli. The walls of each alveolus and its surrounding capillaries are thin. This allows the oxygen to enter the blood freely at the same time that carbon dioxide goes in the other direction, from the blood to the lungs to be breathed out.

In order for your respiratory system to work properly, it is important that the bronchi and alveoli are kept clean and free of infection. The hair in the nasal cavity and the cilia in the windpipe help to protect our lungs from much of the dust and harmful bacteria in the air, but they cannot protect us from many other dangers. Traffic fumes, harmful chemicals, and cigarette smoke are just three of the pollutants that easily get into our lungs, but are not so easy to get out. Cigarette smoke, for example, will cover a person's alveoli and bronchi with a thick black tar making it harder to breathe. This tar builds up and also makes it easier for the bronchi to become infected. In addition it becomes more difficult for the heart to receive oxygen-rich blood, and so the person's whole body will suffer.

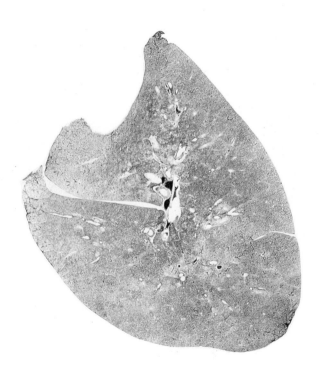

Section of healthy human lung.

Section of a lung covered with deposits of tar, caused by cigarette smoking.

The Digestive System

Food is handled by the digestive system. Starting at the mouth, it is mainly one long winding passage called the alimentary canal. The digestive system may handle as much as 100,000 pounds (45,360 kilograms) of food during an individual's lifetime.

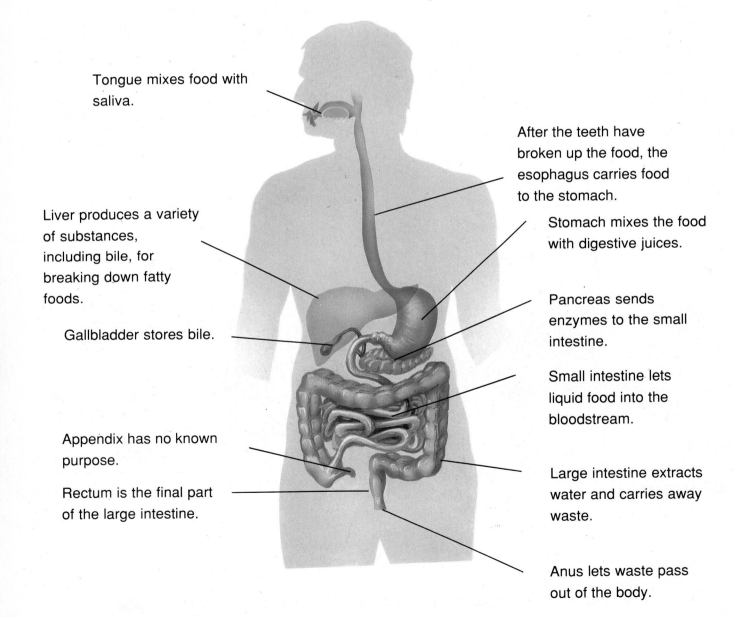

Tongue mixes food with saliva.

Liver produces a variety of substances, including bile, for breaking down fatty foods.

Gallbladder stores bile.

Appendix has no known purpose.

Rectum is the final part of the large intestine.

After the teeth have broken up the food, the esophagus carries food to the stomach.

Stomach mixes the food with digestive juices.

Pancreas sends enzymes to the small intestine.

Small intestine lets liquid food into the bloodstream.

Large intestine extracts water and carries away waste.

Anus lets waste pass out of the body.

Digestion involves breaking down food so that it can enter the bloodstream. The blood carries this broken-down food to all the body tissues. There the food is burned for energy or is used as building blocks to make more cells.

The first act in the digestion of food is chewing. This breaks the food into small pieces and mixes it with saliva, the liquid given off by the mouth. The saliva wets the food, making it easier to swallow. In the saliva is a chemical called an enzyme. The enzyme acts on starchy foods, helping to break them down into sugar, which is easier to digest.

When you smell something good to eat, your mouth "waters." Actually saliva is being produced. This tells you that you are hungry.

The mouth also aids digestion by cooling warm foods and drinks or warming cold ones.

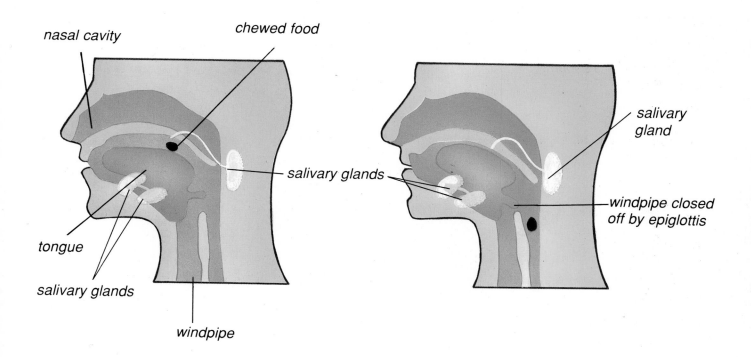

nasal cavity

chewed food

salivary glands

tongue

salivary glands

windpipe

salivary gland

windpipe closed off by epiglottis

Food is broken into little pieces by your teeth. It is rolled around and formed into a ball, or bolus, by your tongue. The bolus is moistened with saliva, which makes it easier to swallow. The saliva contains an enzyme that starts to digest starchy foods.

After food has been chewed, it is swallowed. It passes down a tube called the esophagus, or gullet, by a squeezing movement called peristalsis. The muscles that cause this movement are different from muscles that cause movement of bones. The muscles causing peristalsis are called smooth muscles. You do not have to think to make your smooth muscles work. Your nervous system automatically controls them.

Digestive juices in the stomach include acid, mucus, and more enzymes. The acid and enzymes help break down starches, proteins, and fats in food. The food itself is also mixed by churning movements caused by more smooth muscles in the lining of the stomach.

Mucus helps protect your stomach wall from being burned by the acid. The food, after all this, looks quite different from the way it did on your plate. It looks something like oatmeal and is called chyme.

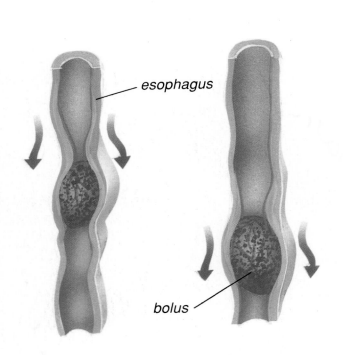

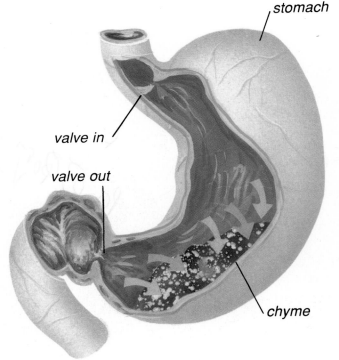

The bolus, the soft mass of chewed food, is forced down your esophagus by a muscular movement called peristalsis. This is done automatically without your thinking about it. The arrows show the direction of muscular movement.

At the bottom of your esophagus, the food bolus passes through a valve into your stomach. Churning movements of your stomach mix the food thoroughly with digestive juices.

The chyme moves from the stomach through a round muscular valve called a sphincter. It then enters a short tube called a duodenum, which is the beginning of the small intestine.

In the duodenum, more digestive juices are mixed with the food. These neutralize the stomach acid and break down the food into even simpler chemicals. One juice comes from a large gland called the pancreas. The pancreas juice contains very powerful enzymes.

Glands in the intestine itself produce other enzymes. All these enzymes work together to complete the chemical breakdown of proteins and starches in the food. A third digestive juice, called bile, is added to this mixture. Bile is made by the liver and it is stored in a small pouch called the gallbladder until it is needed. Bile causes fats to break down into very tiny droplets.

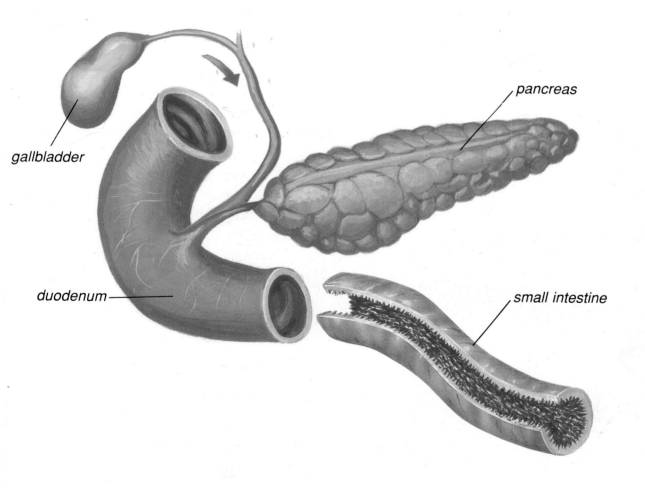

pancreas

gallbladder

duodenum

small intestine

After all this, the food is finally ready to be taken into the bloodstream. Food goes into the bloodstream through the lining of the small intestine.

The walls of the small intestine are lined with tiny, fingerlike projections called villi. (One is called a villus.) These contain blood vessels and lymph ducts.

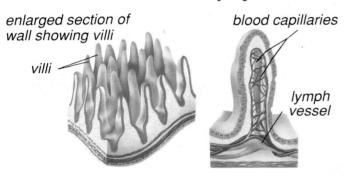

enlarged section of wall showing villi

villi

blood capillaries

lymph vessel

The villi have very thin walls through which the simple chemical compounds (digested food) pass easily into the blood capillaries and lymph vessels. The millions of tiny folds that make up the villi increase the surface through which food passes into the bloodstream.

Once the nourishing food has passed from the villi into the bloodstream and the lymph system, all that is left is water and undigestible parts of food. The leftover material then moves to the large intestine. Some fiber foods cannot be broken down by even the most powerful enzymes. This fiber, however, is useful in maintaining the muscle tone of the large intestine.

The main job of the large intestine is to take back the water your body needs from undigested food. Water passes through the walls of the large intestine and into the blood. The rest of the material leaves the body.

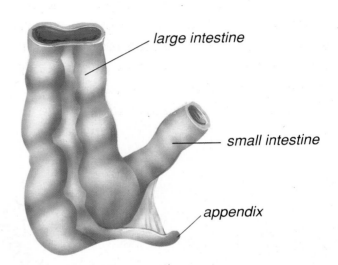

large intestine

small intestine

appendix

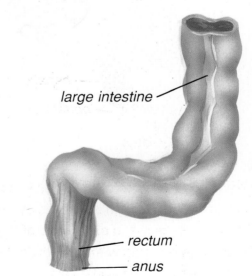

large intestine

rectum

anus

At one end of the large intestine is the appendix. No one really knows what the appendix is for. At the other end of the large intestine is the rectum, where remaining waste escapes the body.

The Liver

When the digested food has entered the bloodstream, it is taken to the liver. The liver is the largest gland in the body. It is dark, reddish brown and has a spongy texture. As part of the digestive system, the liver makes useful substances. Two of these are bile, which helps break down fatty foods, and heparin, which prevents blood from clotting inside blood vessels. The liver is also the main quick energy maker of the body. It changes extra glucose, a kind of sugar, into glycogen, which its tissues can store. Glycogen can be quickly changed back to glucose, to provide energy when it is needed between meals.

The liver also stores important vitamins and iron. Iron is needed to make hemoglobin for blood. The liver breaks down old, worn-out red blood cells, but saves their iron.

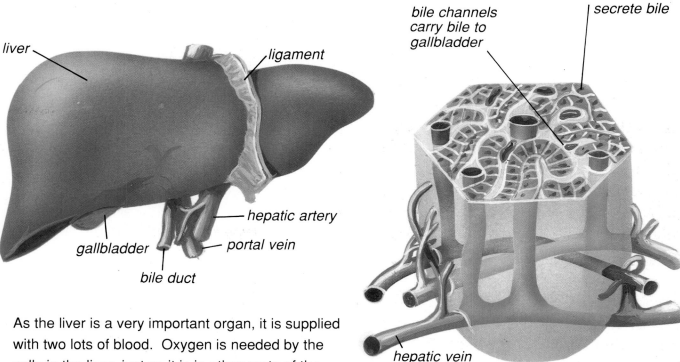

As the liver is a very important organ, it is supplied with two lots of blood. Oxygen is needed by the cells in the liver, just as it is in other parts of the body. The blood is brought by the hepatic artery. Blood also comes to it in the portal vein.

The liver is made up of many small lobules, each well supplied with blood vessels and tiny canals that carry bile to the gallbladder.

Teeth

There are different kinds of teeth for different jobs. The front teeth, called incisors, are used for cutting and slicing. The back teeth, called molars and premolars, have broad, bumpy surfaces for grinding up the food, to make it easier to swallow. Canines are the more pointed teeth between the incisors and the molars. The points of the canines help to pierce and tear food.

Newborn babies have no teeth. By the time a child is two and a half years old, twenty teeth have grown. These are often called milk teeth. They fall out after a few years and are replaced by adult teeth.

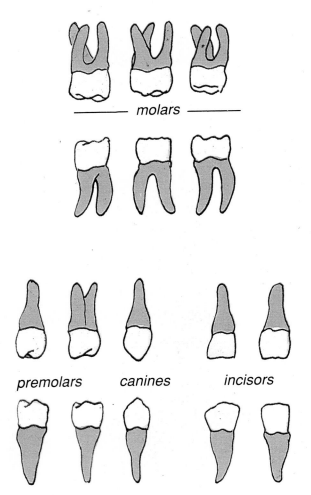

—— molars ——

premolars   canines   incisors

The teeth in the adult's mouth consist of incisors, canines, premolars, and molars.

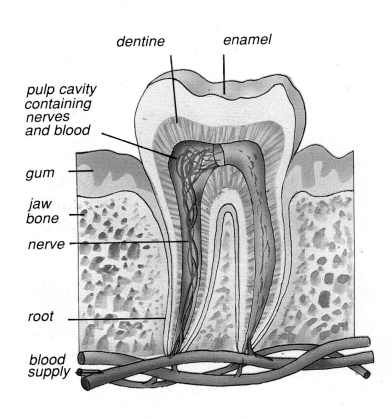

dentine   enamel

pulp cavity containing nerves and blood

gum

jaw bone

nerve

root

blood supply

Teeth break up food so that it can be swallowed more easily. The picture shows the parts of a molar, which grinds food, at the back of the mouth. In front are the incisors and canines, for cutting and tearing food.

Teeth have three parts: the crown, the neck, and the root. The root is anchored to sockets in the bone of the jaws. The neck is surrounded by the gums. The part you can see is the crown, which is covered by shiny enamel. Inside the tooth is a pulp cavity that contains tiny blood vessels and nerves.

Strong teeth are necessary to good health. They should be cleaned often to get rid of bacteria that cause tooth decay. Bacteria feed on pieces of food in the mouth and produce acid. This acid attacks the enamel. After a time a hole forms in the enamel of the tooth. The dentist drills a hole into the tooth to clear away decay and bacteria. The hole is cleaned and then a filling is put into it. The filling, which is hard, takes the place of the missing natural material and prevents further decay.

A wax impression is made of a person's mouth when false teeth have to be fitted. Porcelain and plastic are used for false teeth.

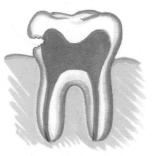

cavity with bacteria

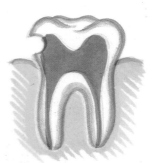

drilled cavity

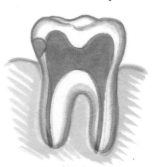

cavity filled

Fillings are usually made of a mixture of silver, tin, and copper.

Fact box

Sometimes your teeth grow crooked. Then, you have to go to a special dentist called an orthodontist. The orthodontist will take careful measurements and decide if you need metal bands, called braces, on your teeth. Braces apply gentle pressure to your teeth which gradually makes them straight.

The Urinary System

We have learned that undigested food leaves the body as solid waste. This waste never enters your blood, but passes right through the alimentary canal. But there are other wastes that must be expelled as well.

When food is burned in cells for energy, carbon dioxide gas is produced. This, as we have seen, leaves through the lungs during respiration. The other waste product from food burning is ammonia, a poison. The liver changes ammonia into a harmless chemical called urea. The blood then carries it to the kidneys, where the urea is filtered out.

The kidneys are two organs at the back of your abdomen, on a level with your waist. Each kidney has over a million tiny filter units called nephrons. An artery, called the renal artery, brings blood to the kidneys. Before the renal artery enters the kidney, it is divided into many capillaries. Where the capillaries come into contact with the nephrons, the urea is filtered out of the blood. Useful materials and the cleaned-up liquid are returned into the bloodstream. In fact, ninety-nine percent of the cleaned liquid goes back into the bloodstream from the kidneys.

The remaining one percent, called urine, travels down tubes called ureters, to the bladder. The urine is stored in the bladder until it is eliminated through another tube, called the urethra. Urine contains many different kinds of waste dissolved in water in addition to urea.

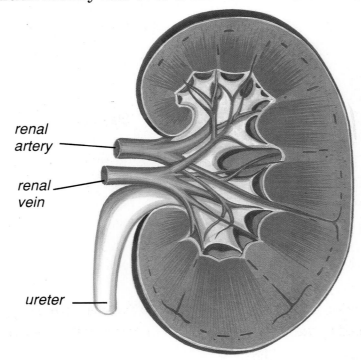

renal artery

renal vein

ureter

Your kidneys hold over a million tiny nephrons that filter urea from the blood to make urine. The urine travels through small tubes to reach two large tubes called ureters. These carry urine to the bladder.

Your body is about two-thirds water. The water must be kept at a constant level. Also, it has to be spread out through all your cells. Every time you eat or drink you take in water. The kidneys control the balance of water. They also control other substances in your body, such as salt. Normally, the more you drink, the more urine your kidneys make.

In hot weather, however, the amount is less. Extra water is needed for perspiration which helps to cool the body down. In cold weather the body needs less water, so more urine is made by the kidneys.

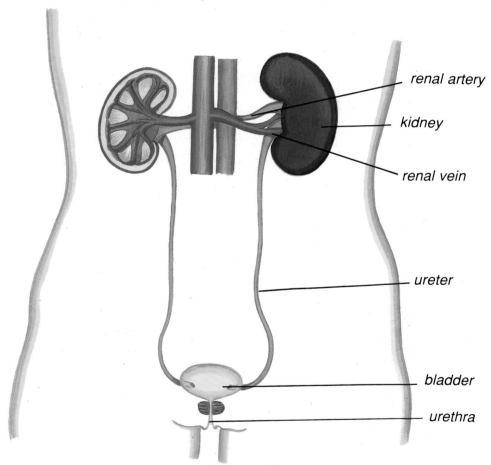

— renal artery

— kidney

— renal vein

— ureter

— bladder

— urethra

The urinary system is one of the body's main systems for getting rid of waste. Urea, water, and mineral salts are excreted by the kidneys through the ureters and the bladder.

The Nervous System

The nervous system is made up of the brain, the spinal cord, and millions of individual nerve cells arranged in bundles and cables or fibers. Together, these parts control your actions and reactions to everything that happens inside your body. They also bring you messages from the outside world.

The brain is the largest concentration of nerve tissue in the body. Its signals to and from the organs and muscles are carried by nerves. Most nerves connect to the brain through the spinal cord, which runs down a series of openings in the vertebrae. Each nerve is also connected to a certain part of the body.

Your nervous system connects to all the parts of your body. Part of the system works automatically – for instance, keeping your lungs breathing and your heart beating. Other nerves go into action when you want to do something, such as clench your fist.

Shown here are two parts of the nervous system – the central nervous system and the peripheral nervous system. The central nervous system consists of the brain and the spinal cord. The peripheral nervous system is made up of sensory nerves, which send messages to the brain from the sense organs. It also includes the nerves, called motor nerves, which take messages back to the glands and muscles.

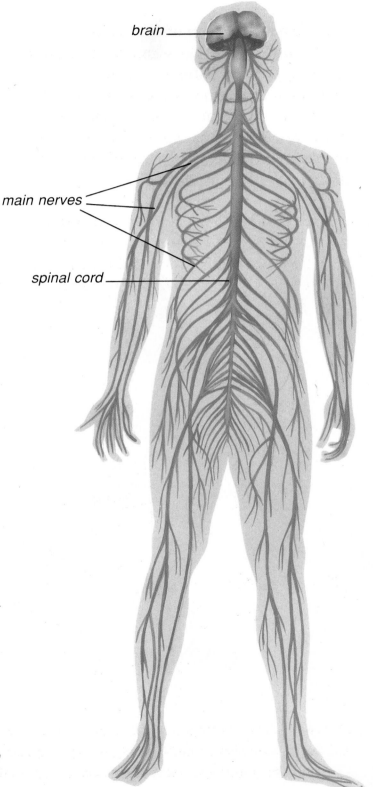

brain

main nerves

spinal cord

Nerves are made up of cells called neurons. Neurons have many threadlike arms called dendrites which receive messages and carry them to the cell. The cell's one long arm, or axon, passes the message on to the dendrites of other cells through electrical currents called impulses.

Sensory nerves have axons of different sizes. Messages travel faster along fat axons than along thin ones. Some axons are very long, such as the one that leads from the base of the spinal cord to the big toe.

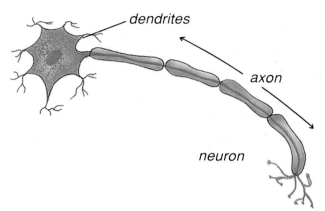

A neuron, or nerve cell, passes electrical impulses along its axon to the next neuron, and so on. Finally, the impulse reaches its goal, such as a muscle or gland.

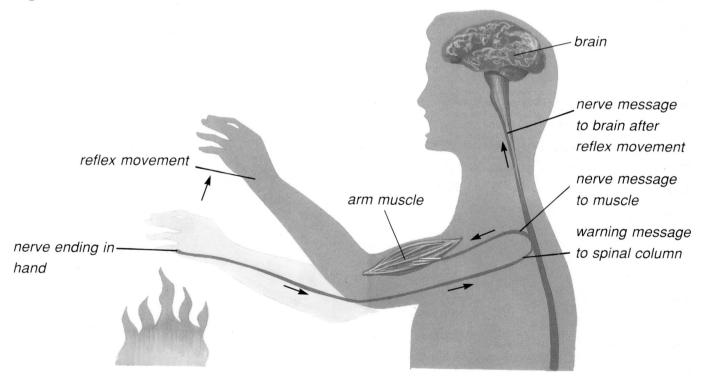

In reflex actions, messages travel to and from the spinal cord without the brain's help. If your hand accidentally touches something hot, it will spring back. A nerve message from your spinal cord tells your muscles to pull your hand out of danger. Only later is your brain notified of the action.

The Autonomic Nervous System

The autonomic nervous system is part of the peripheral nervous system. It controls such things as body temperature, blood pressure, breathing, muscle movements in the alimentary canal, and the manufacture of special substances by the glands. All this is unconscious control, without thinking. But the autonomic nervous system also links with the central nervous system, which is controlled consciously by the brain.

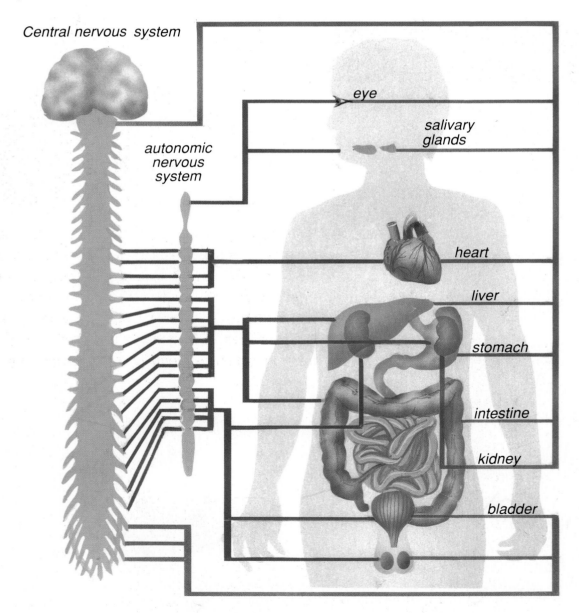

Central nervous system

autonomic nervous system

eye

salivary glands

heart

liver

stomach

intestine

kidney

bladder

Special sensory nerve endings, called receptors, bring the nerve cells information from outside the body. The skin has more receptors than anywhere else in the body. They are especially numerous near the lips, fingers, and soles of the feet. These are the places where the outside world is most likely to make contact with the skin.

There are also receptors in the ears, eyes, and other sense organs.

Fact box

The lips have many nerve endings. This is one reason babies put things into their mouths – to find out what shape they are and what they feel like. People feel sensations differently. One may find the temperature of a bath comfortable, for instance, and another may feel that it is painfully hot.

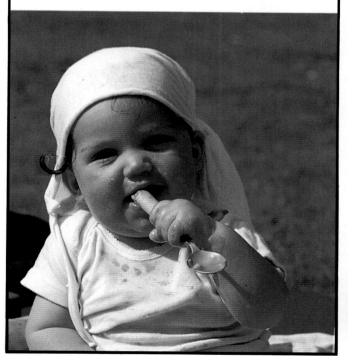

Some receptors found in hairless parts of the body, such as the lips or finger tips, are formed into tiny disks. In other parts of the body, the receptors are wrapped around the base of the fine hairs and respond to any stimulation of the hair. Receptors are influenced by the temperature, which is why our sense of touch seems to be impaired during cold weather.

The Brain

Your brain is the control center, or headquarters, for your body. It is made up of about 10 billion nerve cells. Your brain receives messages and gives instructions for all your activities, whether you are aware of them or not.

There are three main parts of the brain, the largest of which is the cerebrum. Your sense organs send messages to the cerebrum, so that you know what you are seeing, hearing, smelling, feeling, or tasting. The cerebrum controls the movement of your skeletal muscles. It is also the center for thinking, learning,

memory, and feeling emotion.

The cerebellum is the part of the brain that controls balance. The third part, the brain stem, connects the brain to the spinal cord. It coordinates your breathing, digestion, heartbeat, and other important processes.

Most nerves lead into and out of the brain through the spinal cord. Sensory nerves from the eyes, nose, mouth, and ears enter the brain directly from the skull region where these organs are located.

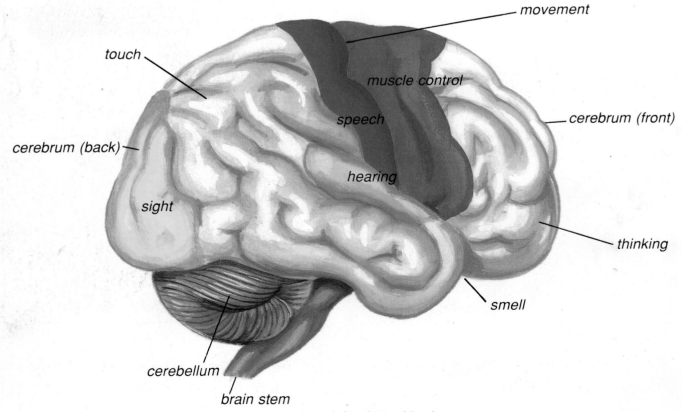

right view of brain

The brain is divided into two sides called hemispheres. The left side of the brain controls the right side of the body. The right side of the brain controls the left side of the body because the nerves to and from the spinal cord cross over in the lower section of the brain.

At birth, your head was large for your body. Your brain weighed about one-tenth of the weight of your body. In an adult, the brain weighs about one-fiftieth of the weight of the body.

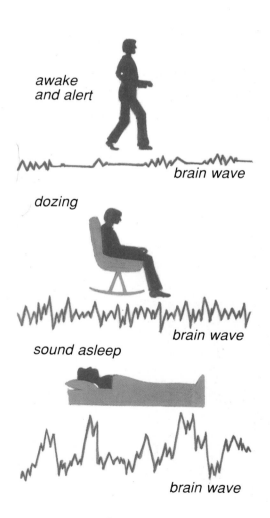

awake and alert

brain wave

dozing

brain wave

sound asleep

brain wave

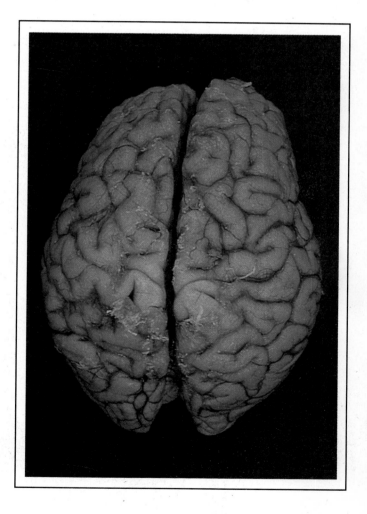

Your brain never sleeps. There are always parts of it that stay active.

Viewed from above, the two cerebral hemispheres of the brain can be seen easily.

Learning and Memory

Thinking is the ability to understand and react properly to the conditions that come up in life. Scientists know how various parts of the brain receive information from the outside. However, they do not know how the brain puts all this information together in a way that makes us more, or less, likely to use it well. There is no question that some people learn more quickly and remember longer than others, but nobody understands exactly how the brain produces what we usually call "intelligence."

There are many kinds of intelligence. Some people learn to do things like writing and spelling very quickly. Others may be better at drawing pictures. All forms of learning are examples of intelligence.

three months

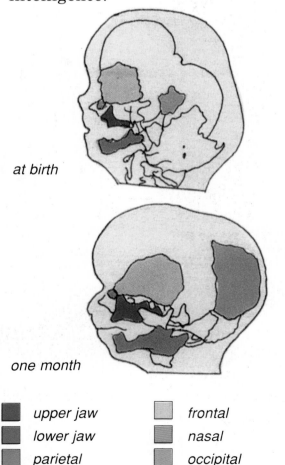

at birth

one month

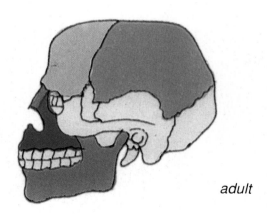

adult

As the brain grows, the skull bones grow to protect it. Intelligence is linked to the number of brain cells and their connections in the cortex (the outer layer of the brain). Humans are the most intelligent mammals, and have the largest brains.

■	upper jaw	■	frontal
■	lower jaw	■	nasal
■	parietal	■	occipital

Your eyes, ears, nose, skin, and tongue bring information to the brain all the time. Your brain stores this information until you need it. This is called memory. There are at least two different stages for memory. One is for recent memories and one for long-term storage of memories.

During your life you learn to do many things. Perhaps you have learned to ride a bike. Your brain will store this information so that you will always know how to ride a bike, even if you don't do it for a long time.

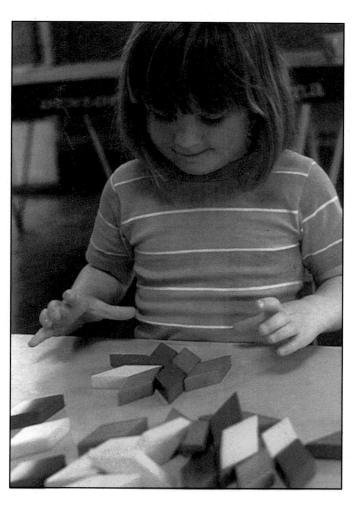

A highly intelligent child will quickly learn how to make shapes from the pieces.

Once you have learned to ride a bicycle, you will probably never forget it.

Speech

A newborn baby does not speak, but it does make sounds. After listening to others speak, a child learns to copy sounds. Usually, by one year of age, a baby can say a few words.

Sounds are made by using flaps of skin called vocal cords. These are at the top of the windpipe. Vocal cords are part of the voice box, called the larynx. Muscles in the throat can push the vocal cords closer together. When air from the lungs is forced through them, they vibrate. Put your fingers gently on the Adam's apple, the small bump at the middle of your neck. Now speak, and you will feel vibrations.

Your mouth shapes the sounds from your voice box into words. Try making the same noise and move your lips, tongue, teeth, and cheeks to see how many different sounds you can make. Usually your vocal cords are opened for quiet breathing. If they are nearly closed, rushing air can make them vibrate to produce a sound. To make high-pitched noises, the vocal cords must be stretched tight. This is done by tilting back the cartilage to which the cords are attached. When the cartilage is tilted forward, the cords are loose and will make low-pitched sounds. The stronger you breathe out through the slit between the cords, the louder the sound will be.

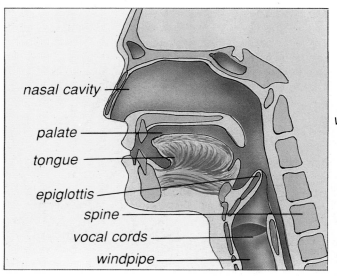

Air forced through the vocal cords in the larynx makes sounds. These sounds are formed into speech by the mouth.

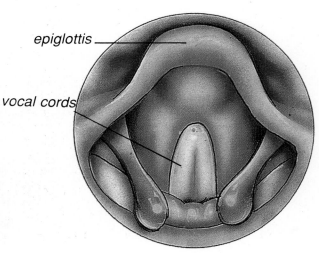

Looking down the throat, the epiglottis is seen as a flap of skin that can drop over the windpipe to close it when food is swallowed.

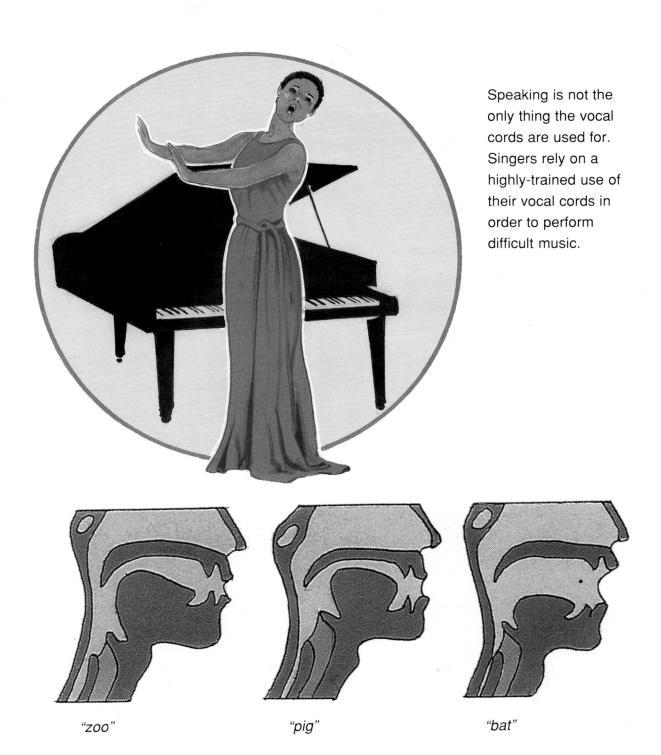

Speaking is not the only thing the vocal cords are used for. Singers rely on a highly-trained use of their vocal cords in order to perform difficult music.

"zoo"   *"pig"*   *"bat"*

The epiglottis, tongue, and mouth are shown making three different words. Children soon learn how to do this correctly.

Taste and Smell

Two senses, taste and smell, work very closely together. Their nerve endings detect particular chemical substances, such as those which give flavor to food.

There are four basic tastes: sweet, sour, salt, and bitter. Nerve endings for each of these tastes are located on different areas of the tongue. These nerve endings are called taste buds. Adults have about 9,000 taste buds. Most are on the tongue. Others are on the roof of the mouth and at the back of the throat. Try tasting a little salt. You will notice that the "salty" taste buds are along the edges of the tongue.

Your sense of smell can help your sense of taste and your digestion at the same time. When your nose picks up pleasant chemical signals from food, it sends signals to the brain. These signals cause your mouth to make saliva, to wet and soften food for swallowing. As food material dissolves, sensory nerves send messages to the brain about the taste and texture of the food. This in turn causes more saliva to pour into the mouth.

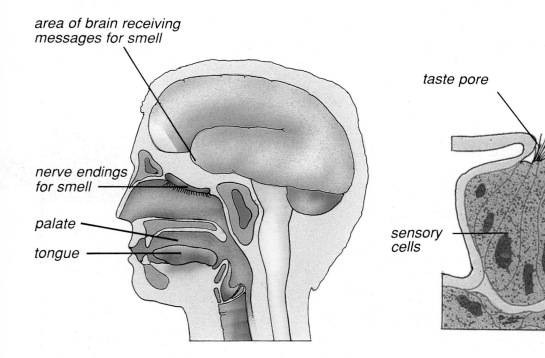

area of brain receiving messages for smell

nerve endings for smell

palate

tongue

taste pore

hairs

sensory cells

Nerve cells at the back of the nose are able to detect chemical substances in the air.

This is a taste bud. The number of taste buds a person has decreases as a person grows older.

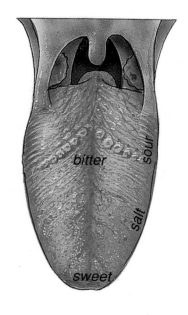

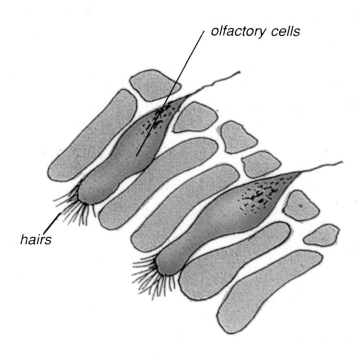

Different areas of the tongue detect the four different tastes of food — sweet, sour, salt, and bitter. The flavors of food are a combination of their taste and smell.

These are nerve cells for smell. A well-trained nose can detect up to 10,000 different smells. The brain remembers them so we can recall them later.

You will notice that when your nose is blocked by a cold, food seems less interesting and flavorful. Your sense of smell works with your sense of taste to give you the full flavor. Nerve endings for smell are located high up in your nostrils. When a smell reaches your nose, you sniff to get more of the scent to the smelling, or olfactory, cells. These cells not only tell you about good things, like food, but they also tell you when you smell something dangerous, such as a harmful gas. Olfactory cells are very sensitive and can detect many odors.

Fact box

Toothpaste has some detergent in it. This keeps your taste buds from sensing sweetness for a while. If you drink orange juice after brushing your teeth, it tastes nasty. Because of the toothpaste, you can only taste the bitter and sour tastes of the juice and none of the sweet.

Sight and the Eye

We see things because light falls on them. Light bounces off objects and moves into each eye, where special light-sensitive cells detect it and send information to the brain about what we see.

Light first goes through a clear layer called the cornea, at the front of the eye. It enters the pupil, the smaller black center of the colored iris. The pupil is surrounded by a ring of muscle that can tighten or relax to match the amount of light that is available. This is why your pupils are larger in dim light.

The lens behind the iris focuses light on the back of the eye, or retina, to give

sharpness of vision. There, light-sensitive cells called rods and cones are packed together. They are connected to the brain by a cablelike structure, the optic nerve.

Rods can detect very small amounts of light, allowing some vision even in semi-darkness. Cones are the color detectors. Some cones see red, some see green, and others blue. The brain combines these messages to recognize the whole range of colors. Cones do not work well in dim light. This is why it is hard to tell colors when you are out at night.

The hollow eye is filled with a thick fluid called vitreous humor. It gives the eye its

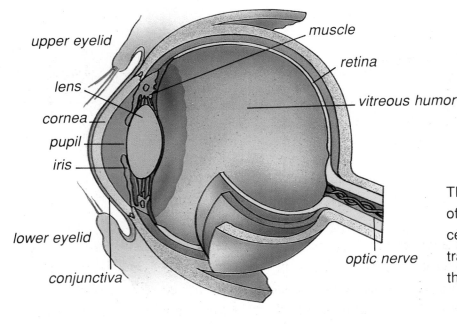

upper eyelid
muscle
retina
lens
vitreous humor
cornea
pupil
iris
lower eyelid
optic nerve
conjunctiva

These are various parts of the eye. The hollow center contains a transparent fluid called the vitreous humor.

rounded shape so it can easily turn in its socket when you look around. Each eye sees things from a slightly different angle. You can see this if you look at an object first with one eye, and then with the other. The brain uses this information to judge distance. The eyes turn in to look at nearby things and look straight ahead at distant things.

On the outside, the "white" of the eye is protected by a membrane, called the conjunctiva, which also covers the inside of the eyelids. The conjunctiva acts as a shield which is wiped by the eyelids when you blink. The eyelashes help keep dust off the conjunctiva, and the eye is lubricated by moisture from the tear ducts.

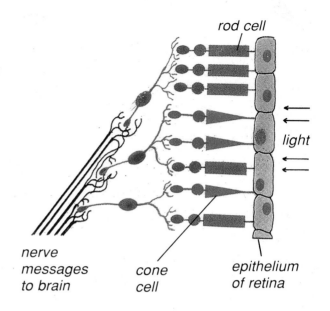

A layer of transparent cells covers the retina. Behind it are rod and cone cells, which react to light. Rods are sensitive to black and white. Cones are sensitive to colors.

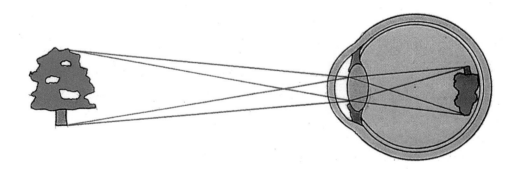

Rays of light travel through the pupil and are bent by the lens to form an upside-down and reversed left to right picture on the retina. The cells of the retina are sensitive to light. They send information to the brain about the color and shape of the image. When the message reaches the brain, the pictures are turned right side up and unreversed.

Hearing and Balance

The ear is an amazing and delicate organ. It can hear all the sounds an orchestra makes — at the same time! It hears loudness and softness, high and low notes. From the signals it sends to your brain, you can tell the sound of each instrument.

Sound is carried through the air by invisible ripples called sound waves. When these strike other objects, they cause them to vibrate, or move back and forth. The motion is so small that you cannot see it. But it is what allows you to hear.

Your outer ear acts as a sound catcher, or funnel. It sends the sound waves down a short tube to a tight flap of skin called the eardrum. The waves cause the eardrum to vibrate, just like the top of a drum.

The vibrations cause three little bones in your middle ear to move. The movements are sent by the bones to another tight membrane, called the oval window. This window leads to the inner ear. In the inner ear is a maze, called the labyrinth, that is hollow and filled with fluid. At the end of the labyrinth is a spiral coiled tube, called the cochlea. Inside the cochlea is another membrane, which floats in liquid. The membrane contains some of the nerve endings of the auditory nerve.

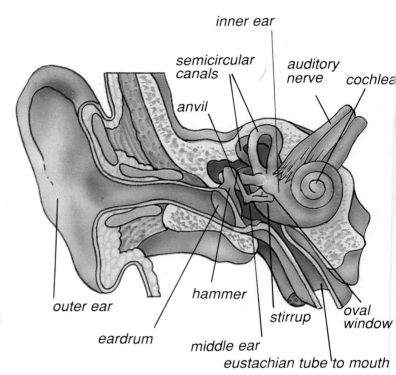

The ear has three parts: outer, middle, and inner.

There are up to 20,000 nerve endings in each ear. When the vibrations from the eardrum, ear bones, and oval window reach the cochlea, they set its liquid vibrating. Depending on the kind of vibrations, the nerve endings receive different kinds of messages about the sound that is coming in. These messages are relayed to the brain by the main auditory nerve.

The brain tells you what the vibrations are: people talking, traffic moving, or a fly buzzing around your head. The brain can tell the difference between vibrations, if they are loud enough. If sounds are too loud, they can damage the eardrum.

Air pressure inside the ear is adjusted by the eustachian tube. This narrow tube runs from inside your ear to the back of your throat. When you swallow, chew, or yawn, the entrance to the tube opens and air travels in or out of your middle ear. This makes the air pressure on both sides of your eardrum the same. In other words, the air pressure inside your head matches the air pressure outside it. This allows your eardrum to vibrate easily so you can hear properly. If the outside pressure changes too quickly, it is uncomfortable to your ears. When you take off in an airplane, this sometimes happens. You can help to equalize the pressure on your ears by swallowing often.

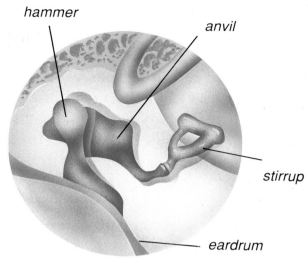

hammer

anvil

stirrup

eardrum

Vibrations in the eardrum move the bones of the middle ear (the smallest bones in the body). These are called the hammer, anvil, and stirrup because of their shapes. The stirrup vibrates the oval window, another sensitive membrane.

The workings of the ear are delicate and must be kept clean. Your body handles this by making a sticky material called earwax. Dust and dirt stick to the wax and do not go any further into your ear.

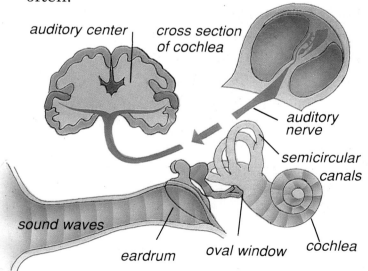

auditory center

cross section of cochlea

auditory nerve

semicircular canals

sound waves

eardrum

oval window

cochlea

Vibrations are passed on from the oval window to the liquid inside the cochlea of the inner ear. When sound waves reach the cochlea, the movements are picked up by nerve endings and are sent to the brain. The brain receives the waves as sound.

The ears have another job to do. In addition to hearing, they are the main organs of balance. In another part of the liquid-filled labyrinth are three hollow, curved tubes, called semicircular canals. The canals point outward in three directions. When you move your head, the liquid in one of the canals will move. A message goes to your brain about the position of your head to help you to keep your balance. If you whirl around and around, your semicircular canals become confused. Then you get dizzy and lose your balance.

The Sense of Touch

There are several kinds of nerve endings in your skin for the sense of touch. Scientists know of at least five different kinds, but there may be even more than that. What is certain is that some parts of your body are more sensitive to touch than others. These parts probably contain more nerve endings. Your fingertips, for example, are very sensitive to touch. This is because they have more nerve endings than anywhere else on the body.

In addition to the fingertips, the lips, tongue, hands, and feet are the most sensitive. When you touch something with your finger, you feel it almost immediately. The nerve endings in your finger have sent an electrical signal to your brain by way of the spinal cord. Your brain distinguishes between the different nerve messages such as itch, cold, heat, touch, pressure, and pain. The brain also registers the strength of the signal.

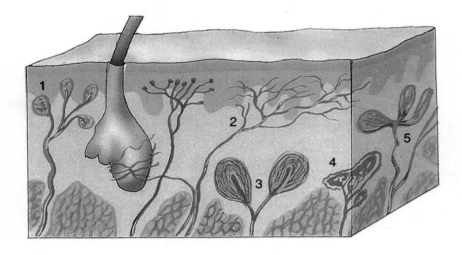

The skin is a major sense organ with nerve endings sensitive to cold, pain, pressure, heat, and touch.

This illustration shows five different nerve endings.

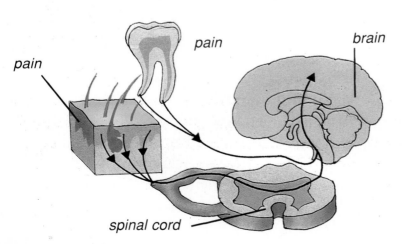

Most sensations from the skin and deeper tissues of your body travel to the brain by way of the spinal cord, except for sensations in the head. A toothache, for example, has a direct nerve route from the jaws to the brain.

The sense of touch is important for your survival. Your skin tells you much more about the things you touch than just the shape and texture. Sometimes you feel only a light touch, such as when you walk barefoot on a lawn. The grass presses evenly on the soles of your feet. When you step on sharp stones, the edges of the stones press harder on your feet. If the pressure becomes too great, your feet begin to hurt. This is because the pressure sets off special nerve endings deep in your skin. This is your sense of pain warning you that your body may be in danger of being damaged.

The skin also provides other kinds of information about the environment. It tells you whether it is hot or cold, wet or dry. Some types of heat are enjoyable, as in a warm bath. But other kinds can cause pain. Nerves in the skin let you know which ones are more painful.

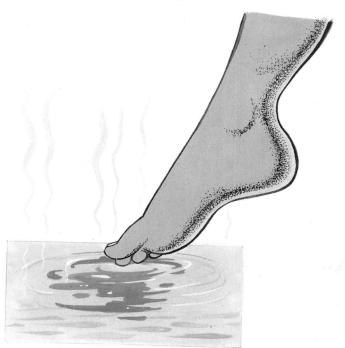

Our feet have to be well protected from pain as we put pressure on our feet more than any other part of our body. Therefore the skin on the soles of our feet is thicker than on any other part. Even so, the nerve endings are sensitive enough to let us know when our feet are in danger from, for example, intense heat or a stony surface.

Our nerves also tell us when heat and cold are pleasurable. For example, most of us like a warm bath. And when the weather is very hot, we like to feel the cooling breeze from a fan.

Skin, Hair, and Nails

Skin is the largest organ in the body. The skin of an adult, for example, covers about twenty-two square feet (about two square meters). The skin covers most of your body and forms the lining of your nose, mouth, and throat. Skin is also found down through your lungs, stomach, and intestines.

The skin has two main layers. The outer layer is the epidermis and the inner layer is the dermis. There is also a layer of soft, fatty tissue below the dermis, called the subcutaneous layer. It cushions the skin layers to protect them from everyday strain.

In the epidermis, new cells are constantly growing from below, pushing older cells slowly to the surface. As these older cells move outward, they become filled with a tough material called keratin. Keratin helps the outer layer of skin keep water inside the body where it is needed. When they reach the surface, the now-dead skin cells are shed harmlessly.

The epidermis also produces melanin, a pigment that gives hair and skin its color. Skin exposed to the sun darkens because it produces more melanin.

The dermis contains blood vessels, nerve endings, sweat glands, and oil glands. It also has small pockets called follicles, from which hairs grow.

The tubes of the sweat glands extend down through the epidermis to their base in the dermis where they coil around themselves. Sweat is mostly water, but a small quantity of chemicals in it gives it a salty taste. The oil glands keep the epidermis from losing its flexibility, or from drying out. The oil produced can mingle with dirt in the pores and clog them up if a person does not wash.

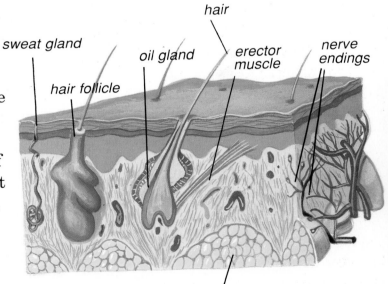

sweat gland · hair follicle · oil gland · hair · erector muscle · nerve endings · subcutaneous fat

Oil glands lubricate the hair to prevent it from breaking. Blood vessels bring food so that the hair can grow. A muscle attached to the hair follicle can make the hair stand on end.

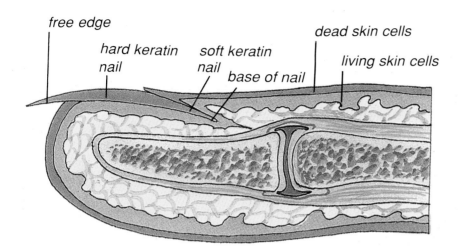

free edge

hard keratin nail   soft keratin nail   base of nail

dead skin cells

living skin cells

The main part of the nail is dead and that is why you do not feel any pain when it is cut. The base of the nail is the growing part and it receives a supply of blood containing food.

A hair grows when cells at the base of a follicle divide and push the hair up. Only the cells at the root are living. The part of the hair you can see is made up of dead cells filled with keratin. They no longer have a blood supply.

After about two years, the cells in the follicle stop dividing. After a few months' rest, the cells begin to divide again and a new hair grows, pushing out the old hair. Most people lose about fifty hairs a day.

Like hair, most of a nail is made of dead tissue filled with keratin. Nails grow from the base, the part that is joined to the finger or toe. As a nail grows, it is pushed out along the surface to the end of each finger or toe. If a nail is damaged, a new one grows back in a short time.

Both hair and nails grow at different rates. The hair in a man's beard, for example, grows more quickly than anywhere else on his body. The nails on the hand you use for writing grow more quickly, because frequent use brings more blood to the hand and blood provides food for growth. For the same reason, fingernails grow more quickly than toenails.

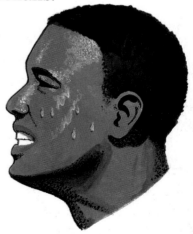

The sweat glands in the skin also get rid of waste water. The flow of sweat is greater in hot weather, when evaporation of moisture is needed to cool the body.

The Endocrine System

Chemicals called hormones travel through your body in your bloodstream. There are more than thirty different hormones, each one with a different job. Some have long-lasting jobs, like those involved with growing up. Others do jobs that go on all the time, like adjusting the amounts of water and salt in the body.

Hormones are made by the endocrine glands. One of these, the pituitary gland, controls body growth. If the pituitary makes too much growth hormone, a child may become a giant. If there is too little, a child might become a dwarf. The pituitary gland is about the size of a pea. It is attached to the underside of the brain. The pituitary makes many hormones, some of which control the actions of other endocrine glands. It is controlled by a part of the brain called the hypothalamus.

The pancreas makes insulin. Insulin is a hormone that controls the amount of glucose (sugar) in your blood. If the pancreas does not make enough insulin, there is too much sugar in the blood. Then the person becomes ill with a sickness called diabetes.

Sex hormones control the ability to have children. In women, sex hormones in glands called the ovaries control the cycle of egg production. In men, sex hormones control the amount of sperm made in glands called the testes. (One is called a testis.) Few of these hormones are made before a person is a teenager.

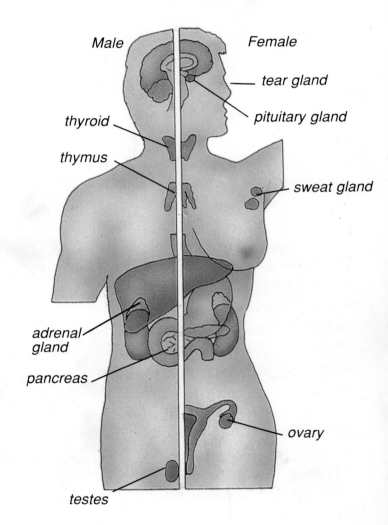

Male   Female
tear gland
thyroid   pituitary gland
thymus
sweat gland
adrenal gland
pancreas
ovary
testes

Here are some of the glands in the body. Endocrine glands make hormones inside the body. Exocrine glands, like the tear and sweat glands, have openings (ducts) to the outside of the body.

The thyroid gland controls the chemical actions in the body that break down food into energy. The thyroid is in your neck, at the front of your windpipe. Hormones from this gland control the rate at which energy is produced in the cells and are necessary for healthy development in newborn babies. Adults with too little thyroid hormones are tired and slow. If they have too much, they become overactive.

Attached to the thyroid are your four parathyroid glands. These help control the amount of calcium in your blood and, together with a well-balanced diet, the minerals in your bones.

Your adrenal glands, located on top of the kidneys, make a number of hormones. One of these, called aldosterone, controls the level of salt in the body. Another, called adrenaline, speeds up some of the body's activities at special times. If you are frightened or angry, the adrenal glands will release adrenaline into the blood. The adrenaline quickly changes stored food into sugar for energy. It makes your heart beat faster. This sends more blood to your muscles. You breathe more quickly, so you get more oxygen into your bloodstream. All this prepares you for action. If you are in danger, you are able to protect yourself or run quickly to escape.

Behind the breastbone, between the

lungs, is the thymus gland. The thymus gland is especially important in babies and young people. It influences the activities of disease-fighting white blood cells called lymphocytes.

The picture shows what happens when either too much or too little growth hormone is produced by the body. The giant has too much of the growth hormone; the dwarf has too little.

The Reproductive System

Babies are born through the activities of the reproductive system. Most other systems in the body are the same in men and women, but in the reproductive system, there are differences.

A man's testes make millions of cells called sperm. A woman has two ovaries, which make eggs, or ova. (One egg is called an ovum.) It takes one sperm and one ovum to make a fertilized egg, which starts the growth of a new baby. The baby grows inside a chamber in the woman's body called the uterus, or womb.

About once a month, an egg is released from the woman's ovaries. The lining of the uterus becomes thick with blood in preparation for a baby. If the egg is not fertilized, the lining comes off and goes out of the body through a passage called the vagina. This is called menstruation.

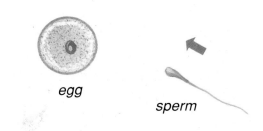

egg

sperm

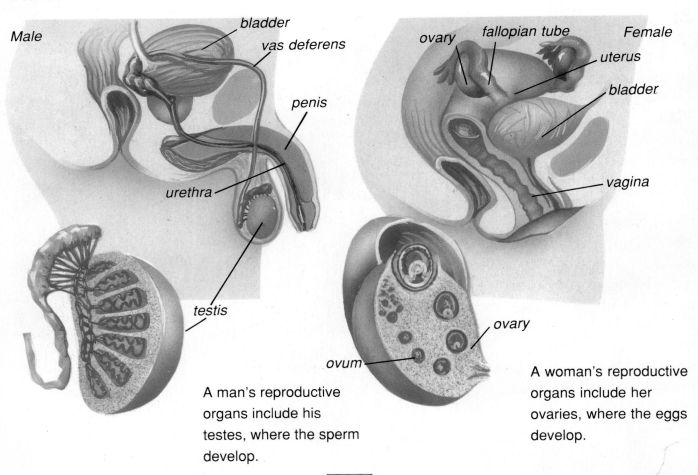

Male

bladder

vas deferens

penis

urethra

testis

A man's reproductive organs include his testes, where the sperm develop.

ovary   fallopian tube   Female

uterus

bladder

vagina

ovum

ovary

A woman's reproductive organs include her ovaries, where the eggs develop.

On its way to the uterus, the egg travels from the ovary through the fallopian tube, or oviduct. In order for an egg to become fertilized, it must come together with a sperm at this time.

Sperm leaves the man's body through a tube called the vas deferens which leads to the urethra in the penis. Though they are cells, sperm can "swim" by wriggling their tails. Millions of sperm swim through the vagina and uterus on their way to meet the egg. Most do not live long enough to reach the oviduct where the egg is waiting. Only one will be able to enter the egg's outer membrane and fertilize it.

When a sperm succeeds in fertilizing an egg, it sheds its tail and the nucleus of the sperm cell joins the nucleus inside the egg. The fertilized egg then travels to the uterus where it develops into a baby. The development of a baby takes about nine months.

Stages in Pregnancy

4th week

8th week

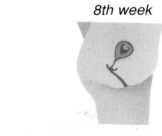

3rd month

6th month

9th month

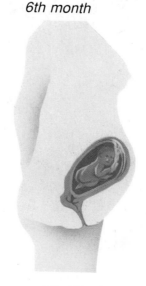

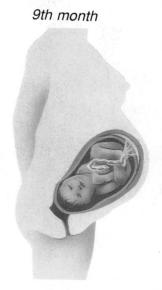

Growing Up

The human body changes in size and shape throughout life. It starts as a single cell, called a fertilized egg. This cell divides and multiplies. After nine months the baby is ready to be born. After birth, there are many quick changes as the baby grows. During childhood, the body continues to grow, but not as quickly. When a person becomes an adult, growth stops.

Not all parts of the body grow the same amount. A baby's head and body are large compared to its short arms and legs. Over the years, the arms and legs grow more quickly than the head.

A newborn baby can find and suck milk. The baby will get all the nourishment it needs from its mother's milk, or from a bottle of milk. A newborn baby can also clutch anything that touches its palm. Otherwise the baby has little control over its muscles. After about six weeks the baby can lift its head. At about six months, the baby can sit up. Babies begin to crawl at about ten months. They take their first steps before they are a year and a half old.

By the time a child is six years old, he or she can walk, talk, throw, run, and begin to read and write. Between six and twelve years of age, a child loses the milk teeth and gets most of the permanent teeth. Later, the child begins to become

an adult during a period called puberty. Puberty begins for a girl at about eleven to fourteen years of age. The girl begins to menstruate and her body shape changes to that of a woman. A boy begins puberty usually at about fourteen years of age. Hair begins to grow on formerly hairless parts of his body and his voice deepens.

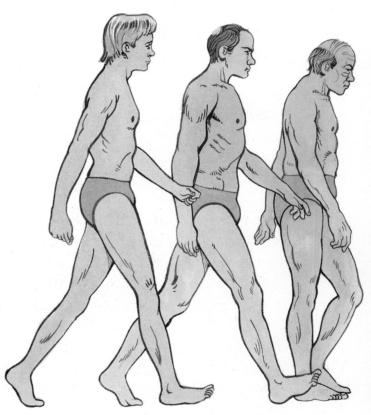

In their early teens boys change into men and girls into women. The bodies of adult men and women do not change greatly until they are old.

Growing Older

As you get older, parts of your body change. An adult's body is not only larger than a child's, it is shaped differently. For instance, young people have smooth skin. When they get older, the skin gets creased and wrinkled. Compared with the more muscular bodies of adults, children's bodies are rounder and softer. Frequently, older people are far-sighted, seeing things better when they are some distance away.

Most people are fully grown when they are twenty years old, although their muscles have not yet reached full development.

By thirty, the muscles have reached their peak of strength. From thirty to forty they gradually begin to weaken. People also begin to notice the first signs of growing old.

During middle age (from forty to fifty years old), there are some changes in appearance. Some people may put on weight and men may begin to lose their hair. A few wrinkles may show up on the skin.

From fifty to sixty the body's internal organs show signs of growing old. The heart will probably not beat as quickly. The number of nerve cells in the brain has fallen. People do not hear so well.

From sixty to seventy years of age, the skin gets more wrinkled. The body now is not able to repair damage as quickly as it used to. People are more likely to get sick, although those that took care of their bodies when young may stay healthier well into old age. Most people shrink a little at this age. They may be as much as two inches shorter than they were at twenty. This happens because the disks between the vertebrae shrink as do the muscles that help us to stand upright. Hair turns gray or white when the body no longer makes enough of the pigment that produces hair color.

These photographs show how former British Prime Minister Winston Churchill's features matured from age 12, to ages 30 and 70.

Why You Are You

Most children look something like their parents. You might have "your mother's eyes" or "your father's nose." Your parents have features that resemble those of their parents. If you have children, they will look something like you. This passing on of physical traits from parents to children is called heredity.

Inside the nucleus of each cell are twenty-three pairs of tiny, threadlike structures called chromosomes. Half of each pair is inherited, or passed on to you, from your mother and half from your father. An exact copy of these chromosomes is passed to every cell in your body.

Chromosomes carry thousands of instructions called genes. The genes carry information that makes you different from everyone else. Genes determine many things about how you look: the color of your hair, skin, and eyes; the shape of your nose; how tall you are. It usually takes a gene from each member of a chromosome pair to determine exactly how a given feature (such as eye color) comes out. Often, several pairs of genes are necessary for a single trait to show up properly.

The way chromosome pairs are inherited happens by chance. This is why you look something like your parents, but not exactly. You have a new combination of

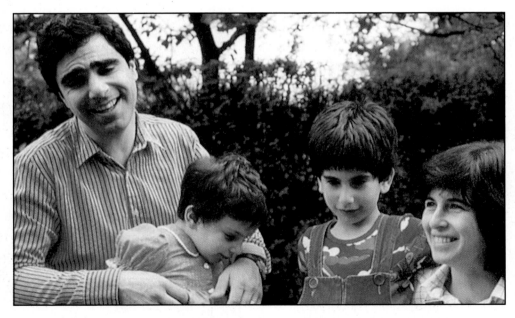

This family photograph shows the similarities between members of a family, due to the influence of related genetic material. Both the children look like their parents – they have their dark hair and eyes.

genes, totally unique to you. You inherit some traits from your parents and also some from earlier generations that may not even show up in your parents. Some genes may be "hidden" or not expressed in physical features, but they never disappear.

Genes also carry the information that decides whether you are a boy or girl. Out of the twenty-three pairs of chromosomes, there is one pair in males that is made up of chromosomes that look different. One is called the X chromosome, and one is called Y. Females have two X chromosomes.

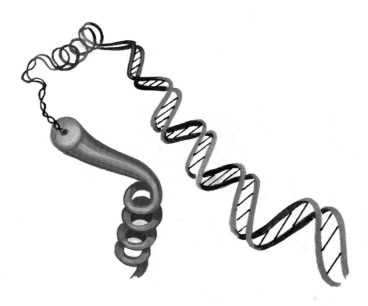

This picture shows an enlarged section of DNA (deoxyribonucleic acid). This is contained within every gene and is the blueprint for new life.

Once in about eighty-nine births, a set of twins will be born. Twins may be identical or fraternal. Fraternal twins are produced when two eggs are released at the same time and each is fertilized separately. Each of these twins has a different chromosome combination, so they are no more alike than two brothers or sisters born at different times. They may be the same sex or different.

Identical twins start off with one egg. When the egg is fertilized, it divides itself into two cells. The cells then divide into four until an entire ball of cells develops. Identical twins are produced when the ball of cells splits into two at an early stage. Each part then goes on to develop into a separate baby. These twins are exactly alike and always of the same sex because they both have the same genetic makeup.

Sometimes people are born with disabilities. These are often caused by faulty chromosomes. Babies born with Down's syndrome, for example, have forty-seven chromosomes in their cells instead of forty-six. One of the chromosome pairs consists of three instead of two chromosomes. These children are mentally handicapped and also have physical disabilities.

Food Types, Vitamins, and Minerals

Your body needs regular supplies of food. Different types of food do different jobs, such as giving you energy or helping you grow. To stay healthy you need a good balance of all kinds of food.

Carbohydrates are for energy and body building. You can eat carbohydrates in the form of sugary food, like fruit or jam, or you can eat them in the form of starch such as potatoes, rice, and bread. Starch is broken down inside your body into a sugar called glucose.

Foods rich in carbohydrates make quick energy, but the energy doesn't last very long. If there is too much glucose for immediate use in the body, it is converted into a substance called glycogen and stored in your liver and muscles. It may also be converted into fat. Too much sugary food, like soft drinks, is also bad for your teeth.

Protein is important in making body tissue. When you are growing, you need a great deal of protein to build more tissue. As an adult, you need protein to keep these tissues healthy. Protein foods include lean meat, milk, cheese, eggs, fish, peas, and beans. The faster you are growing, the more protein you need.

Like carbohydrates, foods rich in fats provide energy. Fats are also essential to the proper working of your nervous system. In addition, fat is stored in your skin and other body tissues to keep you warm. However, too much fat leads to problems. Fats come from meat, milk, butter, vegetable oils, and nuts.

Different vitamins are found in the following foods:

Vitamin A: liver, eggs, milk, vegetables. Vitamin A is important to your skin, and

Carbohydrate foods include sugar, bread, pastry, potatoes, and rice.

Meat, eggs, and milk are some foods that are rich in protein.

Foods high in fat include fatty meats, fried foods, and butter.

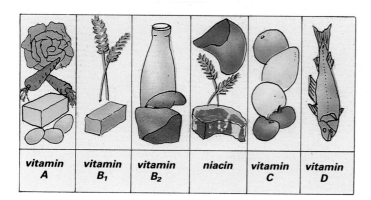

| vitamin A | vitamin B₁ | vitamin B₂ | niacin | vitamin C | vitamin D |

Vitamins are found in many foods. Sometimes cooking can destroy them. If necessary, you can take vitamins in tablet form. We need vitamins to stay healthy.

your eyes, especially for seeing in the dark.

B Vitamins: liver, yeast, milk, eggs, whole wheat bread, vegetables.
There are several different B Vitamins, which are necessary for energy production in all your cells, nerves, and skin.

Niacin is an important vitamin that your body needs. It is found in meats and cereals and is a member of the B Vitamins group.

Vitamin C: fruit and fresh green vegetables.
Vitamin C is necessary for blood vessels, gums, and healing wounds.

Vitamin D: fish oils, eggs, milk, butter, sunlight.
Vitamin D is necessary for strong bones and teeth.

Besides these, there are several other important minerals. We need about twenty different minerals in our diet. Calcium and phosphorus, found in milk and cheese, help make your bones and teeth strong. Your red blood cells need iron. It is found in liver and green vegetables. You also need some sodium chloride or salt. However, too much salt can make your tissues hold onto too much water, which may result in high blood pressure.

Fact box

Fiber, or roughage, is also important in our diet. The main source of fiber is in cellulose, a type of carbohydrate. It is found in vegetables, fruit, and whole wheat. Fiber is valuable because it is bulky. This helps make the muscles of your intestine work efficiently.
Water is necessary for us to stay healthy. We get water not only from drinks, but in certain foods. Lettuce, for instance, is ninety percent water.

Calories and Exercise

Regular exercise is important to health. Your muscles need exercise to stay strong and your joints need exercise to stay flexible. Exercise also helps your breathing and blood circulation.

An athlete's body is strong, firm, and flexible. The exercise during training removes excess fat, and builds muscle tissue. Even if you do not wish to train for track and field, you can find some form of exercise that will keep your body fit.

Regular exercise is good for health. People who work at jobs that make it necessary for them to sit at desks all day need to plan special exercise times.

Exercise offers many benefits to your body. Some exercises are good for your stamina. Stamina is the ability to keep doing something for a long time without tiring. Even walking up a hill may be a strain for someone who is out of shape. Such a person may gasp for breath and his or her heart may beat much faster than usual. The better your physical condition, the more exercise you can do and the better you feel.

Your muscles are never completely relaxed. Even when you are not moving, there are muscles contracting to keep you upright. This constant state of low tension is known as muscle tone. Exercise will help maintain a good level of muscle tone.

The energy you get from food is measured in calories. There must be a balance between how many calories you take in and how many you burn off. People who are very active need to eat a lot of food. A lumberjack needs more food than an office worker. You do not need as many calories to keep your body working while you are watching television as you do when you are playing basketball. Even if you take in only a few more calories than you can use up, your body will store the extra calories as fat, and you will gain weight.

Here are a number of exercises. This chart shows what benefits they offer and how much. 0 means no effect and 10 means excellent.

There are 414 calories in an average-size piece of apple pie. To burn off the calories taken in from eating the piece of pie you could do one of the following:

Chop wood for one hour.
Play tennis for one hour and ten minutes.
Walk for two hours.
Sleep for seven hours.

Sport	stamina	flexibility	strength
Backpacking	7	5	7
Badminton	5	7	5
Ballet	7	10	9
Basketball	10	9	5
Cycling	10	3	5
Gymnastics	5	10	7
Hockey	7	7	7
Jazz Dancing	7	10	5
Jogging	10	3	5
Judo	3	10	5
Soccer	7	7	7
Swimming	10	7	10
Tennis	5	7	5
Walking	3	0	1
Weightlifting	0	0	10

Dealing with Diseases and Disorders

Organisms that cause disease enter the body in several ways. Many are in the air that we breathe. Single cells called bacteria (one is called a bacterium) enter the body in food and drinks. They can also get in through cuts in the skin.

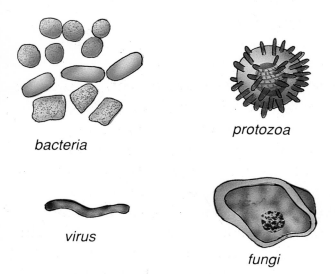

bacteria

protozoa

virus

fungi

A variety of organisms cause disease in the human body.

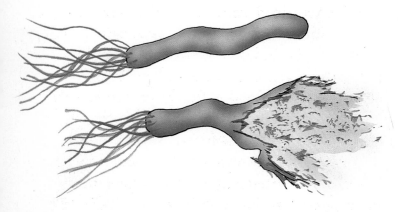

Antibiotics destroy healthy bacteria by breaking down their cell walls.

Medical science helps us to stay well through vaccinations. These make your body immune without getting the disease. The substances that cause the disease are produced in the laboratory. Then the dead or very weak bacteria are injected into your body. This makes your body produce antibodies against the disease and you are protected from it in the future.

When you catch a disease, the body has several natural ways to fight it. The most important are the white blood cells. Some of these destroy harmful bacteria. Others make antibodies that fight attackers. When you have an infection, more white cells are formed than usual. This sometimes makes your glands swell. (You can feel them easily in your neck.) Once your white cells have produced an antibody against a particular disease, they can make it again very quickly when necessary. This is why you do not get certain diseases, such as measles, more than once. You become immune, or protected.

Like all living cells, bacteria reproduce by dividing. A disease may be caused by harmful bacteria damaging your tissues or by the poisons some bacteria make. Bacterial diseases include tuberculosis, typhoid, pneumonia, whooping cough, tonsillitis, tetanus, and certain kinds of food poisoning.

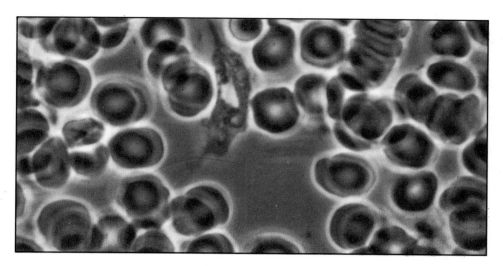

This photograph shows harmful bacteria being swallowed up and destroyed by a white blood cell in the center. Many red blood cells are present.

In 1928, a scientist named Alexander Fleming found that a substance in green mold could kill bacteria. Fleming named the substance penicillin, after a mold that made it. Penicillin is used to treat several infections. Penicillin and similar drugs are called antibiotics. Antibiotics can kill or stop the growth of many of the bacteria that cause disease.

A virus is made of materials carrying genetic instructions inside a protein coat. It can only reproduce itself in a living organism. If a virus invades your cells, it takes them over. It uses your cells to multiply itself. This changes your cells and sometimes leads to disease. One serious disease caused by a virus is polio. It causes a fever and, later, paralysis. At one time, this was a disease suffered by many people, but in the 1950s an American scientist named Jonas Salk developed a polio vaccine. So many people were immunized with this vaccine that fewer people suffer with it now.

Other diseases caused by viruses include the common cold, the flu, measles, chicken pox, and the mumps. These diseases are spread by people who already have the virus. They breathe, sneeze, or cough out the infectious viruses and another person breathes them in. This is why people with certain diseases are kept away from others. Diseases that are passed from one person to another are called contagious diseases.

AIDS (Acquired Immune Deficiency Syndrome) is a recently discovered disease. The virus destroys the body's ability to fight disease by attacking certain white blood cells. With the body's immune system weakened or destroyed, disease-causing organisms are able to enter easily. Scientists believe that the AIDS virus must enter the bloodstream for a person to become infected. Although many scientists are working on a cure for AIDS, so far none has been found.

In the United States, cancer is the second largest cause of death. (Heart disease is number one.) A cancer is an uncontrolled growth of cells. Normally, cells divide and multiply according to strict controls. When a person has cancer, some cells multiply wildly out of control. A group of cancer cells is called a tumor. The multiplying cancer cells damage healthy tissue.

Cancer cells can travel through the body, spreading the disease by starting new tumors. Cancers can effect any part of the body. The most common forms of cancer are those in the lungs, breasts, large intestine, skin, and blood (also known as leukemia).

When they are discovered early, many cancers can be cured. Doctors use various treatments, including operations to remove the tumor as well as radiation, strong drugs, and chemicals to kill the cancerous cells. Scientists are always working on new cures for cancer.

Heart disease is another major disease. It is not usually caused by an invading virus or bacterium, but through a defect in the way the body works. Such diseases are called degenerative. A common cause of heart disease is a thrombosis, or blood clot in a vessel. Such a clot causes damage to areas of heart muscle.

Sometimes the skin is attacked by a fungus, such as athlete's foot or ringworm. Such diseases cause soreness and irritation. Creams or powders are rubbed onto the skin to kill fungus.

Eczema is a skin disease that causes itching. Eczema is not contagious. It is due to different things in different people. Nervous people sometimes suffer from eczema, and so do some people with food allergies.

Accidents are a major cause of injury. Most accidents happen at home, on the roads, or at work. Young people and old people are most at risk from accidents.

When the skin is broken by a cut, germs can get in and an infection can start. Cuts should be cleaned and bandaged. Bandaging, and pressing down on the bandaged cut, also helps to slow down blood loss in deep cuts. Cuts on or near main arteries are dangerous. These need immediate attention. Otherwise too much blood will be lost in a short time.

Normally, blood cells cannot escape from blood vessels. If the skin has been cut, the blood begins to leak out of the broken vessel. When this happens, a blood clot forms.

Bruises are caused when tiny blood vessels under the skin (capillaries) are damaged. Bruises show up as dark patches under the skin where the blood collects.

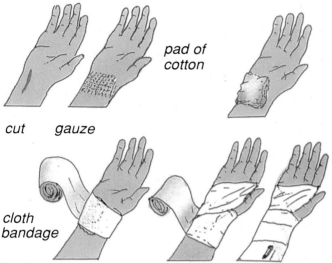

This is how a doctor might bandage a large cut to slow the flow of blood.

Certain plants can produce skin rashes. Poison ivy and poison oak contain substances that cause an itchy rash when you come into contact with the plant.

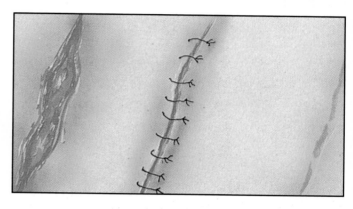

If a cut is large, doctors use stitches to join the two pieces of skin together. When the cut has healed, a scar will sometimes remain.

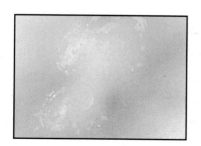

Very hot substances burn the skin. Pouring cold water on the burn will help. If the burn is not too serious, the redness or blister will soon go away. In severe cases, doctors may place skin from other parts of the body on the burned area, where it will grow into a healthy new surface.

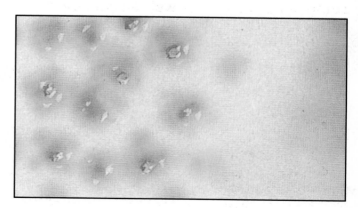

Sometimes rashes, red bumps, and pimples show up due to an infection or irritation. Heat causes rashes in some people.

Hospitals

Sometimes it is necessary for sick people to go to hospitals. Hospitals have special equipment used by doctors and nurses who work there to cure sick people.

There are operating rooms for people needing operations. X-ray equipment takes pictures of the body under the skin and shows where bones are broken or where there are diseases like cancer. There are laboratories where blood is tested and samples from other parts of the body are examined to detect disease.

Many hospitals have extensive laboratory facilities to help diagnose and treat diseases.

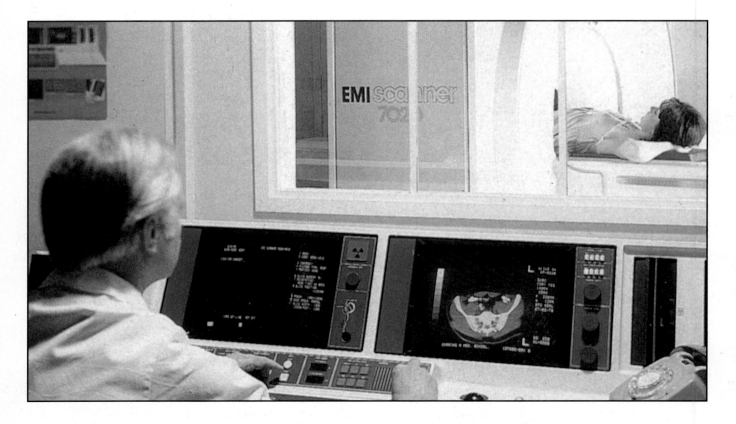

Many types of scanners are used to look at "slices" of various parts of the body. A picture is projected onto a screen so that the doctor can look for signs of disease.

If you are sick and have to go to the hospital, the doctors and nurses will do their best to make you happy and comfortable, as well as helping you to feel better.

Many hospitals have intensive care units. People who are seriously ill are treated in these sections by special nurses and doctors. Complicated machinery helps in preserving life and reporting to the nurses and doctors on the patient's condition. If people come to hospitals with infectious diseases, they are put into isolation. This keeps them from mixing with other patients who might catch their disease.

Psychiatric hospitals have doctors and nurses who are trained to deal with mentally ill patients.

Clinics are places for people who need treatment but do not need to stay overnight. People who are recovering from crippling accidents may go to physical therapy clinics that help them to use their bodies again in a normal fashion.

Helping the Disabled

Sometimes people suffer with illnesses that keep them from moving normally. Medical science has found ways to assist these people.

If someone should lose their leg, for instance, doctors can fit that person with an artificial leg, which will allow the patient to walk. Artificial body parts are called prostheses. The same signals from the brain that normally move the joints can be used to move the artificial limb.

Arthritis is a disease which causes pain and swelling of the joints. There are several kinds of arthritis. Osteoarthritis is most common. It causes pain and limits movement in the larger, load-bearing joints such as hips and knees. Rheumatoid arthritis also causes great pain. It usually begins in people twenty to forty years old, in the small joints of the hands and feet. Sometimes the hands become twisted and useless if the tendons are affected. If arthritis attacks the hip, a person can have trouble moving. Sometimes the worn-out hip can be replaced with an artificial one.

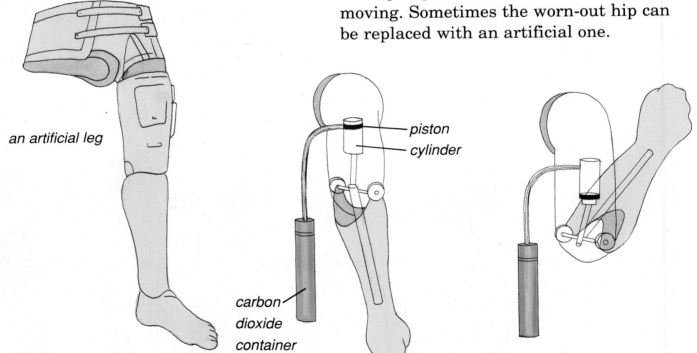

an artificial leg

piston

cylinder

carbon dioxide container

Many people who have lost limbs in accidents can be helped by replacements. These people can then lead more normal lives.

One way of stimulating artificial limbs to move involves using a carbon dioxide cylinder. Gas pushed into the cylinder forces the piston down, working a lever that moves the arm upward.

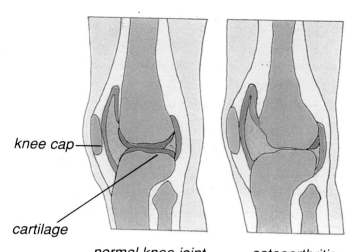

knee cap
cartilage
normal knee joint   osteoarthritis

When osteoarthritis develops, the cartilage between the bones is destroyed. The bones rub against each other, making movement of the joint difficult and painful.

Sometimes disabled people have to live in wheelchairs. There have been many adjustments made for the comfort and convenience of these people. Elevators have been specially designed to make it possible to get up and down stairs. Ramps and hoists are attached to cars so people can get in and out and drive themselves. Inside special cars are hand levers that take the place of foot pedals. Some wheelchairs have motors, so that people can get around without pushing themselves. There are ramps at theaters, at shopping malls, and along curbs of roads and sidewalks for wheelchair riders to use.

There are also sports events for people in wheelchairs. International Olympic games are held with special events for disabled people.

Drugs and Drug Abuse

Doctors often prescribe drugs for us when we are sick. These help us to get better. Other times people take powerful drugs that are not prescribed. These people are drug abusers.

Some people take drugs to change their mood. This is called "getting high." Many of these drugs cause people to become dependent on "getting high." People who can no longer get along in life without drugs are called drug addicts.

Once an addiction to a drug has developed, it is very difficult to break. If the addict has no trace of the drug in the blood, he or she will experience discomfort. This discomfort is called withdrawal. To avoid the discomfort of withdrawal, an addict will continue to take the drug, even though it is dangerous to do so.

Drug abuse is a major problem. Some people try only once, but many continue to take drugs until their physical and mental health are damaged. Certain drugs, like LSD, can have harmful effects long after a one-time use. A person can become addicted to a powerful drug like "crack" on the first try.

Drug addicts may kill themselves by accidentally taking too much of the drug.

There is also a danger of taking deadly drugs that have been manufactured by criminals who do not know or care what they are doing.

Not all dangerous drugs are illegal. Alcohol is a drug called a depressant. It has a powerful effect on the brain. Alcoholics are people who cannot face life without alcohol. They risk damaging their liver and their brain.

Cigarettes contain dangerous drugs. The nicotine is carried by the blood to the brain. It has a harmful effect on the heart and blood circulation. The tar in cigarettes is known to cause lung cancer.

Fact box

Different drugs have different effects on the people who use them. But there are always some negative changes in a person who is becoming an addict. These are some changes caused by addiction:

Irritable behavior.
Loss of appetite.
Inability to concentrate or think
   properly.
Loss of interest in hobbies and sports.
Sneaky or suspicious behavior.
Theft (to pay for drugs).

A mild drug, called caffeine, is found in tea, coffee, and chocolate. Caffeine is a stimulant. It makes people feel more alert. Some people cannot sleep at night if they have consumed it.

Drug abuse is dangerous. If a user takes an overdose, it could be fatal.

Questions and Answers
How fast does the heart beat?

Normally, an adult's heart beats about 70 times a minute. Your heart beats faster when you exercise, because your body needs more food and oxygen to work properly. When you are resting or sleeping, your heart beats slower.
You can feel your heart beating if you rest your fingertips on the inside of your wrist, or on the side of your neck just below your jawbone. This is called your pulse.

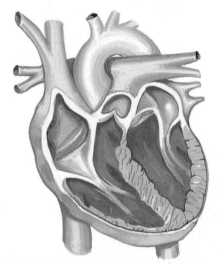

Why do we sweat?

Your body has special reflexes that help keep your temperature as close to normal as possible. When your muscles work hard or the temperature outside is very warm, you need a way to get rid of the extra heat. Sweating brings water from your skin to the surface. As the water evaporates, your skin feels cooler.

Why do we get goose bumps and shiver?

These are two of the ways your body tries to keep you from getting too cold. You have small hairs all over your body. Sometimes when you are cold, the muscles at the root of each hair tighten and the hair stands upright. This causes bumps to appear on your skin.

Goose bumps do not keep you very warm. They work better for animals and birds, who can trap more warm air between their skin and their fur or feathers.

When you shiver, your muscles contract and relax very quickly, over and over again. Because they are working harder, they also produce more heat.

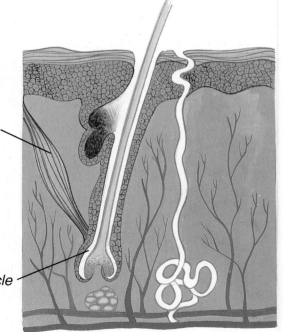

erector muscle

hair follicle

Why does it hurt to hit the funny bone?

The "funny bone" isn't a bone at all. It is really a nerve that stretches across your elbow. Like any nerve, it sends a signal to your brain when it is hit, and you feel pain. Some people think it got its name because it is so close to the humerus, or upper arm bone.

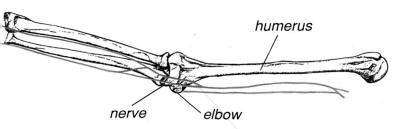

humerus

nerve   elbow

What are the smallest and largest bones in the body?

The largest is the femur, or upper leg bone. The smallest are the three bones of the middle ear, called the hammer, anvil, and stirrup.

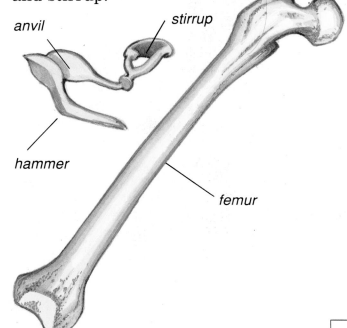

anvil

stirrup

hammer

femur

Why do we sneeze?

Sneezes force harmful particles out of the nose. Some sneezes reach speeds as fast as 100 miles (160 kilometers) an hour!

Sometimes a sneeze is caused by an allergy, or a special sensitivity to dust, animal fur, pollen, or other substance. Colds and viruses can also cause you to sneeze more than you usually do. The viruses attack the lining of your nose, making it irritated or inflamed.

What is sunburn?

Sunburn is caused by ultraviolet rays, invisible parts of sunlight that can burn your skin even on a cloudy day. At first, your skin tries to protect itself from damage by producing more of the pigment melanin.

This is why skin exposed to the sun gets darker, and why light-skinned people burn faster. But even dark-skinned people cannot produce enough melanin to stay completely safe from ultraviolet rays. Overexposure to the sun can cause premature aging and melanoma, also known as skin cancer.

What makes you hiccup?

When you breathe, your diaphragm expands, to let your lungs fill with air, and contracts, to let your lungs expel air. A hiccup is made when your diaphragm contracts more violently than it usually does. It can be caused by eating or drinking too much, and even laughing.

Why do we yawn?

A yawn is a reflex action that brings more oxygen to the body when you are sleepy. It speeds up your blood circulation and stretches your muscles, to help you feel less tired. Once you start a yawn, it is almost impossible to stop it.

What makes hair curly or straight?

The shape of a hair is determined by the shape of the follicle from which it grows. If the follicle is round, the hair will be straight. If it is oval or flat, the hair will grow curly or wavy.

What is your appendix for?

Where your small intestine and large intestine join is your appendix. It has no known use at all in the human body. Some plant eaters, like rabbits, have a much bigger appendix which helps them to digest tough plant food.

Sometimes the appendix can become badly inflamed. This is called appendicitis. If this occurs, the appendix must be removed quickly by doctors in an operation called an appendectomy.

Why do you blink?

Blinking is something you do many times a day, and is one of those body actions controlled by the autonomic nervous system.

When you blink, your eyelids are spreading the fluid produced by the tear glands over the eyeball. Tears do two important things. They keep the eyeball, which moves around a lot and is mainly made up of fluid, lubricated. This lubrication washes away particles that might otherwise hamper the moving eye. Tears also kill bacteria that try to enter the body through the eye.

You will also blink if something has gotten in your eye. This is another automatic response. Hopefully, fluid produced by the tear gland will flush out whatever has gotten into your eye. If it does not, you must always seek assistance to remove the intruder as you could damage your sight if you try to get it out yourself.

How do muscles get bigger?

People who take part in sports and athletics do a lot more exercising and training than most other people. You may have noticed how some athletes, such as football players and sprinters, have very big muscles. To get these bigger muscles, athletes often do special exercises, usually some kind of weight lifting.

When a muscle lifts a heavy weight, the fibers that make up the muscles doing most of the work contract. If they lift a heavy enough weight enough times, the contracting fibers react to the strain. They add more cells, and become thicker. As the fibers thicken, the muscle becomes bigger.

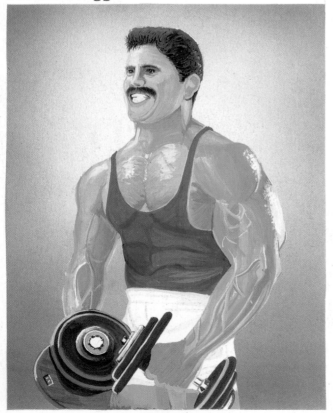

Why are lips pink or red?

Look in the mirror and you will see that your lips are a different color than the rest of your face - a shade of pink or red. Although the lips are on the outside of your body, they are actually part of your throat and the inside of your mouth. They are made of the same mix of mucous membrane and muscle. Their color should be about the same as the inside of your mouth.

What part of your body changes least as you grow old?

Older people develop wrinkles in their skin and get gray hair as they age. But different parts of the body show these changes differently.

One factor in these differences is what kind of work a person does. Someone who has spent much of their life working outdoors, such as a farmer, often has more wrinkly skin than an office worker, because over time the sun can age the skin more rapidly.

Yet one part of the body usually changes very little on the outside. It looks much the same on a person aged sixty as someone aged twenty. It is your ear. For this reason the Federal Bureau of Investigation (FBI) photographs a person's right ear for their records.

What are navels for?

During the time a baby develops in its mother's womb, it cannot breathe in air. This means it cannot get oxygen to its blood, but without oxygen the developing baby would die. The baby gets its oxygen from the circulatory system of its mother through its umbilical cord. The umbilical cord contains one artery to carry the blood enriched with oxygen into the baby, and two veins that transport it out to become enriched with oxygen again.

When the baby is born, the umbilical cord is easily seen, stuck to the skin over the baby's stomach. Most of the cord is taken off by the nurse. The bit left behind soon dries up and falls off. All that is left is the navel, which some people call the "belly button."

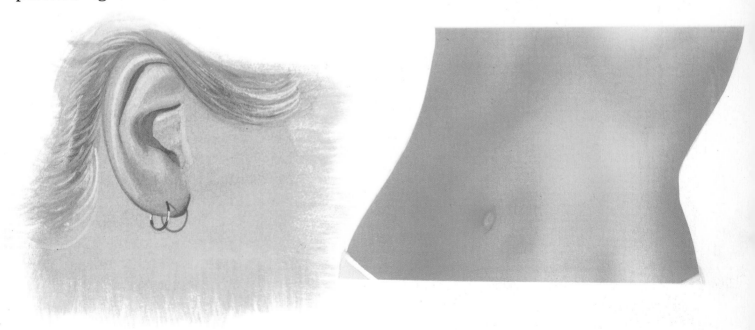

Medical Breakthroughs

Circulation of the blood

Up until the seventeenth century, doctors thought that the blood moved backward and forward, like the tide ebbing and flowing.

The English doctor William Harvey spent many years studying blood circulation, and finally published a new theory that blood was pumped around the body's arteries and veins by the heart.

At the time people did not believe him, and his ideas were very unpopular. But eventually they were widely accepted. Harvey's important work is still studied by medical students today.

William Harvey

Stethoscope

The stethoscope was invented by a French doctor named René Laënnec at the beginning of the nineteenth century. He had tried the usual method of laying his ear to a patient's chest, but then one day he saw some children playing with a log of wood. They tapped at one end and listened at the other.

Laënnec hurried back to his hospital and tried an experiment. He rolled up some paper into a cylinder and used it to listen to a patient's heart. He could hear much more clearly, and later developed a wooden version of his discovery.

Smallpox vaccination

Until the end of the eighteenth century, smallpox was one of the most dreaded of all diseases. It killed many people and left many others with disfiguring scars.

An English doctor named Edward Jenner studied the disease closely and then tested his theories in 1796. He inoculated a healthy human with cowpox, a mild version of the disease. His patient developed an immunity to it, so Jenner then inoculated the patient with smallpox germs, which had no effect. Jenner's method is called "vaccination," which comes from "vacca," the Latin for cow.

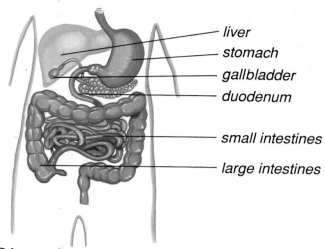

liver
stomach
gallbladder
duodenum

small intestines
large intestines

Aspirin

Aspirin relieves pain and fever, and is one of the most widely used drugs in the world. A French chemist called Charles Gerhardt was the first person to make aspirin. He produced it in 1853, but a German scientist named Heinrich Dreser was the first person to recognize its medical properties. For many centuries people used extract of willow bark to relieve pain. It was effective because it contained a substance which the body can convert into a form of aspirin.

Genetics

A nineteenth century Austrian monk named Gregor Mendel was the first person to understand the way that living things inherit characteristics.

He experimented by breeding thousands of garden pea plants and studying the way that they inherited different characteristics, such as round or wrinkled seeds, and tall or short stems. He published the theory of genes, which are chemicals found in living cells that carry coded instructions passed down from parents.

It is the genes that the girl inherited from her mother that make them look so alike.

Digestion

The Connecticut doctor William Beaumont was the first person to fully understand the workings of the human stomach and digestive system. In 1833 he published theories based on experiments he conducted on a patient with gunshot wounds in the stomach.

Germ theory

In the second half of the nineteenth century, a French scientist called Louis Pasteur discovered the existence of germs – tiny creatures living in the air. He went on to prove that germs were the cause of disease, and developed the theory of inoculation, which means introducing some weak disease germs into the blood. The body fights them and develops a built-in resistance to more severe forms of the disease.

Pasteur's remarkable work opened the way for safe, effective medical treatment.

Germ discovery

Robert Koch, a German surgeon, continued Pasteur's work in the late nineteenth century. He found a method of staining germs with dyes so that they could be seen under a microscope; but his greatest discoveries were in the field of disease. He worked out that a disease could only be caused by one particular germ, and he went on to isolate the germs that cause two of the world's most deadly diseases: tuberculosis and cholera.

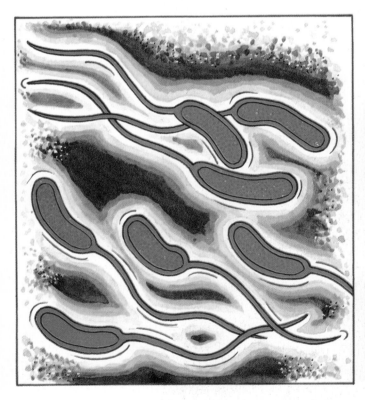

The bacteria that cause cholera – *vibrio cholerae* – were isolated by Robert Koch. The bacteria can contaminate food and water, and cause acute intestinal infection.

Anesthesia

Before operations take place, patients are given anesthetics, which render them unconscious of pain.

In 1800, an Englishman named Sir Humphry Davy suggested that nitrous oxide might be used as an anesthetic. However, the first person brave enough to try it was a U.S. dentist, Horace Wells, in 1844. He used it on himself to have a tooth pulled.

Ether was tried out as an anesthetic by a Georgia doctor named Crawford W. Long and also a Boston dentist named W.T.G. Morton. They share the credit for the discovery.

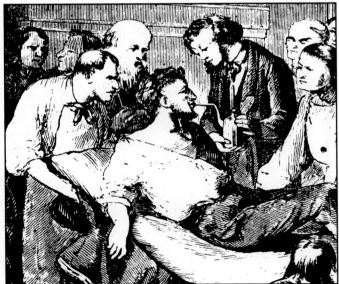

This illustration shows one of the first uses of anesthetics.

Antiseptics

During the late nineteenth century, an English surgeon named Joseph Lister introduced the use of antiseptics during surgery. Antiseptics are chemicals that destroy germs. Before his time, most patients died after operations as a result of infections. Lister's antiseptics were used to clean operating theaters and surgical instruments before use, and many more patients lived as a result.

Yellow fever cure

At the end of the nineteenth century, Cuba's Carlos Finlay published a theory that the dreaded tropical yellow fever disease was spread by mosquitos. The American scientist Walter Reed proved by his experiments that the theory was right, and through his work a way was found to fight the disease by destroying the mosquitos that carry it.

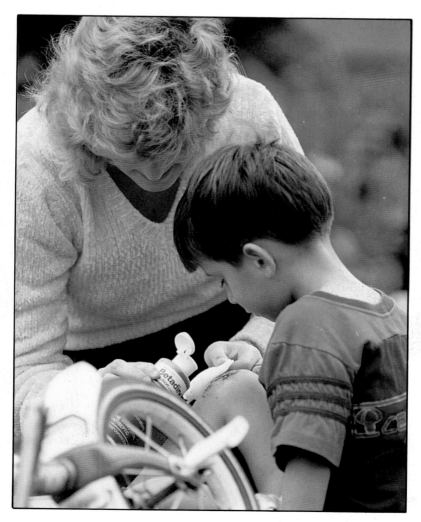

Antiseptics are used to kill germs and prevent the spread of infections.

Polio vaccine

In 1953 the U.S. scientist Jonas Salk developed a vaccine against polio, a wasting disease that particularly affects young children.

Salk carried out his research at the University of Pittsburgh. The first people he injected with his new vaccine were himself and his family.

Albert Sabin carried on the work at the University of Cincinnati. He developed an oral vaccine, which could be taken by mouth.

Lasers

Lasers are concentrated beams of light which can cut through many materials. U.S. physicists first proposed the idea of lasers in 1958, and the U.S. scientist Theodore Maiman built and operated the first laser in 1960.

Concentrated laser beams are now used in surgery to cut through delicate tissues or destroy dangerous cells.

Jonas Salk

During laser surgery for the removal of a mole on the patient's forehead, a protective mask must be worn over the eyes in case the laser beam comes into contact with them and damages the sight.

Heart transplants

The South African Christiaan Barnard studied surgery in Cape Town and at the University of Minnesota. He went on to perform the historic first heart transplant in 1967, replacing a damaged heart with a healthy one.

In 1974, Barnard performed his eleventh heart transplant and achieved another first in medical science. This time, instead of removing the damaged heart, he joined it to a new heart to create a "double pump."

Christiaan Barnard

Gene therapy

Some serious disabilities and diseases are caused by mistakes in an individual's genes. In the past there has been little doctors could do to help people suffering from these. In recent years, though, a better understanding of how genes are made has offered the possibility of a cure.

Gene therapy owes much to the discoveries of James Watson, Francis Crick, and Barbara McClintock. Watson and Crick worked together to discover how DNA, the molecule that is the blueprint for life, carries its instructions to make a gene. McClintock discovered that this blueprint is not permanent. It can in fact be changed, for example, by a microbe called a retrovirus.

In gene therapy, a healthy gene is placed in a retrovirus. A cell is taken from the body of a person suffering from a defective gene. This cell is infected with the retrovirus. The retrovirus inserts a healthy gene into the nucleus of the cell. The cell begins to work correctly. This repaired cell reproduces itself many times, and all these new cells are injected back into the sick person, where it is hoped they will correct the genetic mistake.